W9-CWN-388

Getting Started with Flex™ 4

*Jeanette Stallons, Andrew Shorten,
and Vince Genovese*

O'REILLY®

Beijing · Cambridge · Farnham · Köln · Sebastopol · Tokyo

Getting Started with Flex™ 4

by Jeanette Stallons, Andrew Shorten, and Vince Genovese

Copyright © 2010 Adobe Systems Incorporated. All rights reserved.
Printed in Canada.

Published by O'Reilly Media, Inc., 1005 Gravenstein Highway North, Sebastopol, CA 95472.

O'Reilly books may be purchased for educational, business, or sales promotional use. Online editions are also available for most titles (*http://my.safari booksonline.com*). For more information, contact our corporate/institutional sales department: (800) 998-9938 or *corporate@oreilly.com*.

Editor: Mary Treseler
Copyeditor: Amy Thomson
Production Editor: Adam Zaremba
Proofreader: Sada Preisch
Indexer: Angela Howard
Cover Designer: Karen Montgomery
Interior Designer: David Futato
Illustrator: Robert Romano

Printing History:
> September 2010:   First Edition.

ISBN: 978-0-596-80411-4

[TM]

1283443195

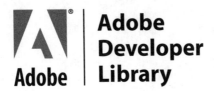

Adobe Developer Library

Adobe Developer Library, a copublishing partnership between O'Reilly Media Inc., and Adobe Systems, Inc., is the authoritative resource for developers using Adobe technologies. These comprehensive resources offer learning solutions to help developers create cutting-edge interactive web applications that can reach virtually anyone on any platform.

With top-quality books and innovative online resources covering the latest tools for rich-Internet application development, the *Adobe Developer Library* delivers expert training straight from the source. Topics include ActionScript, Adobe Flex®, Adobe Flash®, and Adobe Acrobat®.

Get the latest news about books, online resources, and more at *http://adobedeveloperlibrary.com*.

Contents

Preface

If you are curious about Flash Builder and Flex and want to get up to speed in a matter of hours, this book is for you! Hopefully you will be inspired to try Flash Builder and Flex, follow the tutorials to quickly develop an application, and see just how easily you can bring your ideas to life using Flex.

Who Should Read This Book

The short tutorials and sample code in this book are designed to help you evaluate Flash Builder and Flex. Step through the tutorials in sequence and browse the sample code associated with each. The book is designed to be a quick tour of the Flash Builder and Flex world without delving too deeply into any one topic.

The material is targeted at web developers familiar with building applications using PHP, ColdFusion, or Java. If you have a different background or skill set and are interested in learning Flex, check out the "Flex in a Week" video training at *www.adobe.com/devnet/flex/videotraining/*.

To make up for the lack of depth in every area, we provide a collection of resources in Chapter 7 that will help you dive deeper into Flex and Flash Builder.

How This Book Is Organized

Here is a summary of the chapters in the book and what you can expect from each:

Introduction

> This chapter provides a brief introduction to the Flash Platform and showcases some real-world applications and sites that make use of Flex, all of which demonstrate what is possible using Flash Builder and Flex.

Chapter 1, *Build an Application in an Hour*

> This chapter guides you through creating a Flex application that retrieves, displays, and modifies database records.

Chapter 2, *Modify the Database*

> This chapter teaches you how to modify (add, update, and delete) the data in the database from which you retrieved the data in Chapter 1. You create a new EmployeeAdd state, which has an input form for a user to add a new employee to the database.

Chapter 3, *Test and Debug Your Code*

> In this chapter, you learn to test and debug your Flex application.

Chapter 4, *Deploy Your Application to a Web Server*

> In this chapter, you learn to deploy your Flex application to a web server.

Chapter 5, *Change the Appearance of Your Application*

> In this chapter, you learn how to change the appearance of the application you created and deployed using styling and skinning.

Chapter 6, *Add Charts and Graphs*

> This chapter teaches you how to use Flex components and add charts and graphs to your application.

Chapter 7, *Resources for Flex Developers*
> This chapter presents numerous resources for Flex developers, including blogs, forums, podcasts, books, and more.

Conventions Used in This Book

The following typographical conventions are used in this book:

Italic
> Indicates new terms, URLs, email addresses, filenames, file extensions, pathnames, directories, and Unix utilities.

`Constant width`
> Indicates commands, options, switches, variables, attributes, keys, functions, types, classes, namespaces, methods, modules, properties, parameters, values, objects, events, event handlers, XML tags, HTML tags, macros, the contents of files, and the output from commands.

`Constant width bold`
> Shows commands or other text that should be typed literally by the user.

`Constant width italic`
> Shows text that should be replaced with user-supplied values.

NOTE

This signifies a tip, suggestion, or general note.

Using Code Examples

This book is here to help you get your job done. In general, you may use the code in this book in your programs and documentation. You do not need to contact us for permission unless you're reproducing a significant portion of the code. For example, writing a program that uses several chunks of code from this book does not require permission. Selling or distributing a CD-ROM of examples from O'Reilly books does require permission. Answering a question by citing this book and quoting example code does not require permission. Incorporating a significant amount of example code from this book into your product's documentation does require permission.

We appreciate, but do not require, attribution. An attribution usually includes the title, author, publisher, and ISBN. For example: "*Getting Started with Flex 4*, by Jeanette Stallons et al. Copyright 2010 O'Reilly Media, Inc., 978-0-596-80411-4."

If you feel your use of code examples falls outside fair use or the permission given here, feel free to contact us at *permissions@oreilly.com*.

How to Contact Us

Please address comments and questions concerning this book to the publisher:

> O'Reilly Media, Inc.
> 1005 Gravenstein Highway North
> Sebastopol, CA 95472
> 800-998-9938 (in the United States or Canada)
> 707-829-0515 (international or local)
> 707-829-0104 (fax)

We have a web page for this book, where we list errata, examples, and any additional information. You can access this page at:

> *http://oreilly.com/catalog/9780596804114*

To comment or ask technical questions about this book, send email to:

> *bookquestions@oreilly.com*

For more information about our books, conferences, Resource Centers, and the O'Reilly Network, see our website at:

http://oreilly.com

Safari® Books Online

Safari Books Online is an on-demand digital library that lets you easily search over 7,500 technology and creative reference books and videos to find the answers you need quickly.

With a subscription, you can read any page and watch any video from our library online. Read books on your cell phone and mobile devices. Access new titles before they are available for print, and get exclusive access to manuscripts in development and post feedback for the authors. Copy and paste code samples, organize your favorites, download chapters, bookmark key sections, create notes, print out pages, and benefit from tons of other time-saving features.

O'Reilly Media has uploaded this book to the Safari Books Online service. To have full digital access to this book and others on similar topics from O'Reilly and other publishers, sign up for free at *http://my.safaribooksonline.com*.

Acknowledgments

We'd like to acknowledge the help of the Adobe Developer Center and Platform Learning Resources teams in the design and writing of this book. The learning materials that inspired this book were created by Jeanette Stallons, in collaboration with the Adobe team, as an online resource. You can find this material at *www.adobe.com/devnet/flex/testdrive/*.

The scope of the materials online is wider than what you'll find in this book, and we recommend you use both as learning resources as you develop your Flex and Flash Builder skills.

Introduction

If you're curious about Flex and want to get up to speed in a matter of hours, this book is for you!

After providing a brief introduction to the Adobe Flash Platform and showcasing some real-world applications that demonstrate what is possible using Flex, the following chapters walk through building, debugging, and deploying a complete Flex application. You can proceed with each chapter in order or you can explore only the topics that interest you, take a look at the example code, and apply the techniques to your own applications.

Either way, we hope that you enjoy this taste of Flex and that it inspires you to learn more!

First Things First—What Is Flex?

Flex® is an open source software development toolkit for building rich Internet applications (RIAs) on the Flash Platform.

To build a Flex application, you write object-oriented code using the ActionScript 3, MXML, and CSS languages. These languages are easy to learn for programmers from many different backgrounds, such as Java, PHP, C#, HTML, and JavaScript. Flex supports a component-oriented programming model that allows developers to easily assemble applications from components and extend base components to create custom interactions.

The Flex SDK includes a compiler, debugger, and hundreds of ready-to-use components and ActionScript classes that accelerate the development of RIAs. Using these tools from the command line, from build tools such as Ant, or via IDEs from Adobe or third parties, you can compile code into cross-platform applications that run in the browser using Adobe Flash Player or on the desktop with Adobe AIR.

To help software developers rapidly develop applications and content using the Flex framework, Adobe offers an Eclipse-based IDE, Adobe® Flash® Builder™ 4 (formerly Adobe Flex Builder). It includes support for intelligent coding, debugging, and visual design, as well as powerful testing and monitoring tools that speed up development and lead to higher-performing applications. You can find more information on Flash Builder on Adobe's website (*www.adobe.com/products/flashbuilder*).

How Does Flex Work?

Flex source code (in MXML, ActionScript, and CSS files) is compiled into Flash bytecode (a SWF file), which is executed at the client side by the ActionScript Virtual Machine in Adobe Flash Player or Adobe AIR.

To access backend databases and other systems, Flex includes numerous networking APIs that support everything from plain XML, JSON, and SOAP web services to optimized protocols such as Action Message Format (AMF) and Real Time Messaging Protocol (RTMP) (Figure I-1).

Flex applications can leverage the capabilities offered by Adobe Flash Player or Adobe AIR to display complex graphics, handle user interface interactions, and manipulate data (by filtering and sorting, for example) without round-tripping to the server. As a result, Flex applications can deliver an enhanced user experience while being more responsive and easier to use than HTML-based applications.

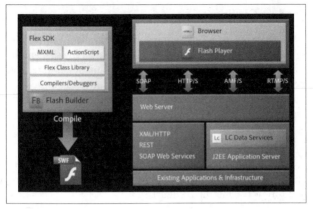

Figure I-1. How Flex works for browser-based applications

What Can You Do with Flex?

You can use Flex to build anything from multimedia-rich consumer experiences to functional line-of-business applications that run behind the firewall. You can use Flex to deliver an entire application experience, or you can embed Flex-based components and widgets within existing HTML websites, including enterprise portals or social networking sites such as Facebook.

In addition to developing browser-based applications that work consistently across Windows, Mac OS X, and Linux operating systems, you can deploy an enhanced, standalone version of your application that makes use of the capabilities available with Adobe AIR. You will also be able to leverage your knowledge of Flex to build applications that work on mobile phones and other Internet-connected devices.

Next, we provide a quick tour of some real-world applications that illustrate the types of experiences you can build with Flex. To learn more about these applications, visit the Flex Showcase (*http://www.flex.org/showcase/*).

Product Configuration

With an ever-increasing amount of prepurchase product research being done online and the phenomenal growth in online transactions, ensuring customers can explore, configure, and personalize products through intuitive and engaging online tools is a key differentiator. This is especially true for complex, high-value products, where thousands, if not millions, of potentially different product configurations can be available.

Mini USA built a product configuration tool that provides a great example of using Flex to present a huge array of choices and combinations to a potential purchaser through an inviting and fun-to-use interface (Figure I-2).

Try it out at *http://miniusa.com/?#/build/configurator/mini-m.*

Figure I-2. Mini USA configuration tool

Consumer Applications

European car manufacturer Fiat selected Flex to develop Eco-Drive, a desktop application for existing Fiat customers who want to improve their driving skills and reduce CO_2 emissions (Figure I-3).

As a desktop application deployed on Adobe AIR, the application isn't constrained by the browser security sandbox. Users can insert a USB key and load car journey data directly into the EcoDrive application, which would be impossible with a browser-based web application.

The application presents the driver with detailed environmental performance of the car, including the CO_2 emission level for each trip. It analyzes the driver's style and then provides tips and recommendations on how to modify that style to achieve CO_2 reductions and save money on fuel.

Download the application at *www.fiat.com/ecodrive/*.

Figure I-3. Fiat EcoDrive application

Media and Publishing

As publishers look to deliver their content to consumers through a variety of different channels, many are leveraging Flex to combine audio, video, images, and text-based information to create digital versions of existing publications.

One such publisher is the *New York Times*. The Times Reader successfully re-creates the newspaper reading experience in a desktop application. Readers can browse through current and archived news, watch video content, adjust the amount of information displayed on the screen based on their preferences, and even complete the interactive daily crossword (Figure I-4).

Download the application at *http://timesreader.nytimes.com/ timesreader/index.html*.

Figure I-4. The New York Times Reader

Education

The ability to seamlessly combine multimedia content in an engaging user experience is also important for online learning applications. New generations of educational tools, which also offer real-time, collaborative multiuser learning, are being built using Flex.

TOTALe is a fully web-based, multiuser language-learning program from Rosetta Stone (Figure I-5). It features online coursework and live sessions with native-language coaches and other students, as well as access to a web-based community with innovative language games. In addition to Flex, this application uses Adobe LiveCycle Collaboration Service, a suite of hosted real-time, multiuser services to provide integrated Voice over IP (VoIP), streaming video, instant messaging, and multiuser rooms.

You can get more information at *www.rosettastone.com/totale*.

Figure I-5. Rosetta Stone web-based tool

Social Networking

With the rise of social networking sites, a variety of tools have emerged to help users manage the information that is important to them.

TweetDeck (Figure I-6) is a great example of a social networking application developed using Flex and deployed on Adobe AIR. TweetDeck is a personal browser for staying in touch with what's happening now, connecting you with your contacts across Twitter, Facebook, MySpace, and LinkedIn. Tweet-Deck nicely demonstrates how Flex applications can connect to a myriad of servers and services and present a single view of data from disparate systems.

Download TweetDeck at *www.tweetdeck.com/desktop/*.

Figure I-6. TweetDeck social networking application

Business Productivity

Some of the most impressive Flex applications available today provide lightweight equivalents to traditional desktop software, such as word processing, presentation authoring, and image manipulation tools.

Adobe launched its own online companion to Adobe Acrobat, called Acrobat.com (Figure I-7), which allows users to create documents, presentations, and tables online; share the latest versions with coworkers; provide feedback; and conduct real-time collaboration in an online meeting room. Built using Flex and leveraging the same infrastructure used to provide the Adobe LiveCycle Collaboration Service, this is a great example of how RIAs are changing the way people work.

Try it out for yourself at *www.acrobat.com/*.

Figure I-7. Adobe Acrobat.com

Data Visualization

Flex includes a comprehensive set of data visualization components that allow you to create reporting and data analysis applications with ease. Better yet, because the framework is extensible, if Flex doesn't include the type of chart or component you require, you can easily create your own.

An impressive example of data visualization comes from Universal Mind's SpatialKey application (Figure I-8), a powerful online location intelligence solution for creating interactive reports and analysis. Flex provides an ideal solution for representing and quickly rendering large amounts of data. For example, hundreds of points on a map can be updated dynamically compared with the display of static points provided by traditional geographic information systems (GIS).

You can get more information at *www.universalmind.com/portfolio/project/spatialkey/*.

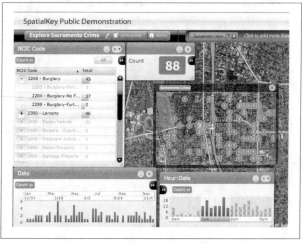

Figure I-8. Universal Mind's SpatialKey application

Financial Services

The financial services sector has produced some of the most sophisticated, high-performance, and data-intensive RIAs in use today. Everything from delivery of real-time market feeds to full-blown stock-trading applications with millisecond response times have been built with Flex.

NASDAQ Market Replay (Figure I-9) is an extremely powerful replay and analysis tool, allowing users to view the consolidated order book and trade data for securities listed on NASDAQ, NYSE, and other regional exchanges at any point in time. By using Adobe AIR to deliver a desktop-based experience, the developers of NASDAQ Market Replay allow users to request and cache volumes of data that they can then analyze even when they're offline.

A case study is available at *www.adobe.com/products/air/*.

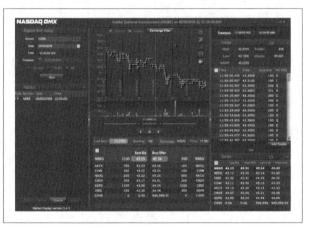

Figure I-9. NASDAQ Market Replay tool

Technologies and Terms Related to Flex Development

There are a host of Flex- and Flash Builder-related technologies and tools that you might want to know about before you start building your Flex application.

Here's a quick rundown of the tools, technologies, and terms that you'll encounter as you explore Flex.

Adobe Flash Platform

The Adobe Flash Platform is an entire family of Adobe technologies you can use to create, run, and provide data to RIAs (in the form of SWF files), including client runtimes, tools, frameworks, servers, and cloud services.

Flash Platform Runtimes

At the center of the Flash Platform are the client runtimes: Adobe Flash Player for the browser and Adobe AIR for outside the browser. The runtimes render applications created on the Flash Platform (in the form of SWF files), allowing users to interact with them.

Adobe Flash Player

Adobe Flash Player is a browser plug-in or Active X control with a rich object model and rendering engine that allows developers to include highly expressive and interactive content in web applications. To include this richer content, you create a SWF file (a compiled bytecode file that Flash Player can render) using developer tools and then reference this SWF file in your HTML page. When the browser parses the HTML page, the Flash Player downloads the SWF file and runs it in the browser window.

Adobe AIR

Adobe AIR is a cross-operating-system runtime and set of tools that allow developers to deploy HTML, Ajax, and Flash Platform applications (SWF files) to the desktop. An emerging design pattern for applications is to deliver a browser-based version for all users and a desktop version for more active or power users.

Applications created on the Flash Platform for the browser use the Flash Player client runtime. These applications have all the benefits of browser-based applications, including anywhere access, easy deployment (no installation necessary), simple updating, and consistency across all operating systems and browsers. They also have all the limitations of browser-based applications, including no offline access and the confines of the browser's security sandbox, which keeps them from interacting with the user's computer outside the browser window. To get the best of both worlds, Adobe introduced Adobe AIR.

You can use Flash Builder to create both web and desktop applications with Flex. If you create both types of applications, you can also share code from separate code libraries. When you compile a Flex application for the desktop, you get a SWF file and an XML file (called the application descriptor file), which includes information about what the container operating system window should look like, what icon should be used for the application on the client computer, and more. When you are ready to deploy, Flash Builder uses a tool called the AIR Development Tool (ADT) to create a release build consisting of an AIR package file, which includes the SWF file, the application descriptor file, assets, and more.

Users must have the Adobe AIR runtime installed to run an AIR application. To provide a more seamless install experience for users, so they can install the application from a web page (instead of having to download and install the AIR runtime and then download and install the AIR application), Adobe provides a default HTML file and *badge.swf* file, which provides a template for letting users click a badge (a framed, customized image button) that checks for and installs the runtime if necessary and then installs the AIR application.

Flash Platform Tools

Adobe offers many tools for creating SWF files, including Flash Builder (formerly Flex Builder), Flash Catalyst, and Flash Professional. Each tool caters to different developer and designer skill sets.

Adobe Flash Builder

Adobe Flash Builder is an Eclipse-based development tool targeted at developers. With this IDE, you use the Flex framework to create SWF files. Flash Builder accelerates Flex application development by providing intelligent code hinting and generation, refactoring, compile-time error checking, interactive step-through debugging, and visual design for laying out and styling user interfaces.

Adobe Flash Catalyst

Adobe Flash Catalyst is a new professional interaction design tool for rapidly creating expressive interfaces and interactive content without writing code. Designers use Flash Catalyst to create the functional user experience and provide the project file to developers who use Flash Builder to add functionality and integrate with servers and services.

Adobe Flash Professional

Adobe Flash Professional CS5 is the industry standard for interactive authoring and delivery of immersive experiences that present consistently across personal computers, mobile devices, and screens of virtually any size and resolution.

You can find more information about each of these tools and the workflows between them on Adobe's website (*http://www .adobe.com/products/flex/workflow/*).

Flash Platform Languages

You create Flex applications using two languages: ActionScript and MXML.

ActionScript is an inheritance-based object-oriented scripting language based on the ECMAScript standard. The latest version, ActionScript 3.0, is based on ECMA-262 4th edition, which was proposed but never approved and published. The syntax and object-oriented features are very similar to Java: you define and extend classes; define and implement interfaces; and use the private, public, protected, and internal (package) namespaces. Unlike Java, in ActionScript you use curly braces inside the package keyword when defining classes, you use the function keyword to declare methods, and you use post-colon data typing instead of the data type prefixes used in Java. Data typing is also optional. You can type everything for IDE code-hinting and compile and runtime type checking, but you can also use dynamic typing when appropriate for flexibility.

MXML is a convenience language; it provides an alternate way to generate ActionScript using a declarative tag-based XML syntax. When you compile an application, the MXML is parsed and converted to ActionScript in memory and then the ActionScript is compiled into bytecode (your SWF). Although you never have to use MXML, developers typically use it to define application interfaces (for layouts, the MXML code is usually more succinct and understandable than the corresponding ActionScript would be) and use ActionScript to write the application logic. Just as you break up your logic into separate ActionScript classes, you also break up your MXML code into separate reusable MXML components.

Servers and Server-Side Technologies

The Adobe Flash Platform provides a number of technologies for enabling communication between Flex applications and server-side applications.

Flex remote procedure calls

Flex applications can communicate with backend servers using either direct socket connections or, more commonly, through HTTP. You can make HTTP requests (to JSP or XML files, RESTful web services, or other server files that return text over HTTP), web service requests (to web services that return SOAP-formatted text over HTTP), or Flash Remoting requests (to methods of server-side classes that return binary AMF over HTTP). When possible, it is advisable to use Flash Remoting, because its binary data transfer format allows applications to load data up to 10 times faster than with the more verbose, text-based formats such as XML, JSON, or SOAP.

Flash Remoting

Flash Remoting MX is a combination of client- and server-side functionality that together provides a call-and-response model for accessing server-side objects from Flash Platform applications as if they were local objects. It provides transparent data transfer between ActionScript and server-side data types, handling the serialization into AMF, deserialization, and data marshaling between the client and the server. Flash Remoting MX uses client-side functionality built into Flash Player and server-side functionality that must be installed on the application server.

Flash Remoting MX is built in on some servers (such as Cold-Fusion and Zend), but must be installed on other servers (via BlazeDS or LiveCycle Data Services on Java EE servers, via WebORB or FluorineFx on .NET servers, via the Zend Framework or AMFPHP on PHP servers, and more).

BlazeDS

You can choose from several different server-side Flash Remoting implementations for Java servers. BlazeDS is a free, open source implementation created by Adobe that provides server-side Java remoting as well as a web messaging technology to push data in real time to Flex applications. The messaging service also allows Flex applications to exchange messages with other nonFlex, JMS-enabled applications.

You can use a combination of the remoting and messaging services to create real-time, data-centric applications. When a user changes some data in this type of Flex application, the data is saved in the database on the server and then pushed out to all the other clients currently accessing the data so users always see the most up-to-date data. To create this type of data synchronization using BlazeDS or a similar technology, you must typically write quite a bit of code to save the data on the server, push the data out to the other clients, and manage any data conflicts. Alternatively, you can use LiveCycle Data Services, which provides much of this functionality for you (see the following section on Adobe LiveCycle Data Services).

You can find more information on BlazeDS at *http://opensource .adobe.com/wiki/display/blazeds/BlazeDS*.

Adobe LiveCycle Data Services

Adobe LiveCycle Data Services is a superset of BlazeDS that provides a complete data infrastructure for enterprise Flex applications. In addition to providing the remoting and messaging services available with BlazeDS, it also provides a data management service that can reduce development and maintenance costs for real-time, data-centric applications.

The data management service automates data synchronization between a Flex application and the middle tier, providing conflict resolution, paging and lazy loading, management of large collections of data and nested data relationships (such as one-to-one and many-to-one associations), integration with Hibernate, and offline data access in AIR applications. You can add many of these advanced data management service features to your applications without writing any server-side code using modeling technologies introduced in LiveCycle Data Services ES2.

LiveCycle Data Services also provides advanced deployment options for maximum scalability, streaming with the RTMP,

PDF generation, portal integration, LiveCycle connectivity, access to developer and enterprise support resources, and more.

You can find more information on Adobe LiveCycle Data Services at *www.adobe.com/products/livecycle/dataservices/*.

Flash Platform Services

Instead of hosting and managing your own data messaging service, you can also use the Collaboration service, which provides real-time collaboration features, including chat, audio, and video. The Collaboration service is one of the Adobe Flash Platform Services, which also include the Distribution service (for distributing, promoting, tracking, and monetizing applications on social networks, mobile devices, and desktops) and the Social service (for integrating with multiple social networks, including Facebook, MySpace, Twitter, Yahoo!, Google, and AOL, using a single ActionScript API).

You can find more information on Flash Platform Services at *www.adobe.com/flashplatform/services/*.

CHAPTER 1

Build an Application in an Hour

In this chapter, you will create a Flex application that retrieves, displays, and modifies database records. Flex applications do not connect directly to remote databases. Instead, you must connect your application to a data service written in your favorite web language (PHP, ColdFusion, Java, or any other server-side web technology). You will build the frontend Flex application; the database and the server-side code to read, add, edit, and delete database records is provided for you as a PHP class, a ColdFusion component, or Java classes. The completed application is shown in Figure 1-1.

Build the User Interface

In this chapter, you will build a Flex project and a Flex application that retrieves data from the database and displays it. The application will display Employee data on one "page" in the application and Department data on another.

The first task is to create a new Flex project for your application server and create the user interface. You'll retrieve data from the server and display it in Chapter 2.

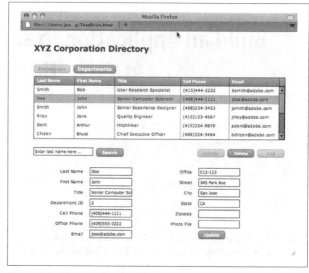

Figure 1-1. The completed application

Step 1: Install the Test Drive Server Files

These files include a database and server-side files to manipulate data in the database. Your Flex application will call methods of one of these server-side files, *EmployeeService*.

Use the following steps to set up PHP:

1. Download and unzip the Test Drive PHP server file from *www.adobe.com/devnet/flex/testdrive/assets/test drive_setup_PHP.zip*. It contains a database and a *Test Drive* folder.

2. Create the `testdrive_db` database on your MySQL installation using the *testdrive_db.sql* file located in the *Database* folder. If you do not have permission to create a database, use the *testdrive_table.sql* file instead to create two tables in an existing database. After you create the database, set user privileges for it.

3. Move the *TestDrive* folder, which contains the PHP service file, to your PHP server.

4. Open */TestDrive/services/EmployeeService.php* in an editor and change the `username`, `password`, `server`, `port`, and `databasename` properties to the correct values for your setup. This class file contains the methods you will call from your Flex application to retrieve, add, update, and delete data.

Use the following steps to set up ColdFusion:

1. Download and unzip the Test Drive ColdFusion server file from *www.adobe.com/devnet/flex/testdrive/assets/testdrive_setup_CF.zip*. It contains a CAR file.

2. In the ColdFusion Administrator, navigate to Packaging & Deployment and deploy the CAR file. In the Deploy Wizard, change the deployment locations to reflect the locations of the *db* and *wwwroot* folders on your server. After deploying, check that you have a new data source called `testdrive_db` and a new folder in *wwwroot* called *TestDrive*.

3. Open */ColdFusion/wwwroot/TestDrive/services/EmployeeService.cfc* in an editor and examine the code. This class file contains the methods you will call from your Flex application to retrieve, add, update, and delete data. The methods have the access argument set to remote so that you can call them from a Flex application.

4. Open */ColdFusion9/wwwroot/WEB-INF/flex/services-config.xml* in an editor. This file is used when calls are made to the server from your application. Locate the `<property-case>` tag and change all three values to `true`, as shown below:

```
<property-case>
    <!-- cfc property names -->
    <force-cfc-lowercase>true
    </force-cfc-lowercase>
    <!-- Query column names -->
    <force-query-lowercase>true
    </force-query-lowercase>
```

```
                <!-- struct keys -->
                <force-struct-lowercase>true
                </force-struct-lowercase>
        </property-case>
```

NOTE

If you are using an earlier version of ColdFusion, your configuration file may not have these tags and you will need to add them. For details, refer to the documentation on using Flash Remoting with your particular server.

---

5. Restart the ColdFusion server.

Use the following steps to set up Java:

1. Download and unzip the Test Drive Java server file from *www.adobe.com/devnet/flex/testdrive/assets/test drive_setup_JAVA.zip*. It contains a WAR file for a web application called *testdrive*.

2. Deploy the WAR file to your web server. It contains the Java classes, an Apache Derby embedded database, and BlazeDS 4 files.

NOTE

BlazeDS 4 is currently in beta. This WAR file contains BlazeDS files from the January 29, 2010, nightly build.

---

3. Open */{your server webapps folder}/testdrive/WEB-INF/src/services/EmployeeService.java* in an editor. This class file contains the methods you will call from your Flex application to retrieve, add, update, and delete data.

---

4. Open */WEB-INF/flex/remoting-config.xml* in an editor and examine the code. This file is used when calls are made to the server from your application. Notice the definition for the destination called employeeService, which points to the `services.EmployeeService` class.

Step 2: Create a New Flex Project

In Flash Builder, select File→New→Flex Project (Figure 1-2). Create a new Flex project called *TestDrive* and store the project files locally. Be sure to specify your application server type and the appropriate web root and root URL for the web application, and validate the configuration (Figure 1-3).

NOTE

If you are using the Flash Builder plug-in in an existing Eclipse installation, you may need to first switch to the Flash perspective.

The project location is where the application source files will be stored. The compiled application will be stored on your application server in the location you specify for the *Output* folder. This folder should be a subfolder of the TestDrive (or testdrive) application you set up on your application server in the previous section.

The following are some example project settings:

Example project settings for PHP:

- Web root: */usr/local/zend/apache2/htdocs*
- Root URL: *http://localhost:10088/*
- Output folder: */usr/local/zend/apache2/htdocs/TestDrive/ TestDrive-debug*

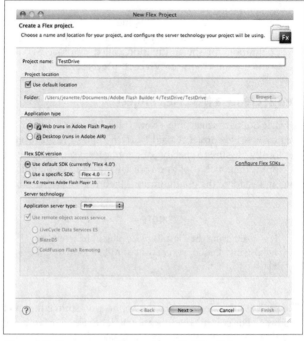

Figure 1-2. Create a new Flex project called TestDrive

Example project settings for ColdFusion; when creating the project, select the ColdFusion Flash Remoting option for remote object access:

- ColdFusion root folder: */Applications/ColdFusion9*
- Web root: */Applications/ColdFusion9/wwwroot*
- Root URL: *http://localhost:8500/*
- Output folder: */Applications/ColdFusion9/wwwroot/Test-Drive/TestDrive-debug*

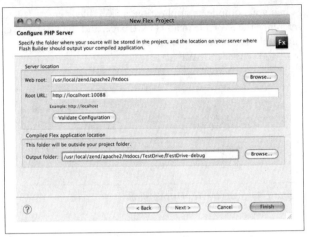

Figure 1-3. Configure your application server and validate it

Example project settings for Java; when creating the project, select the BlazeDS option for remote object access:

- Root folder: */Applications/tomcat/webapps/testdrive*
- Root URL: *http://localhost:8400/testdrive/*
- Context root: *testdrive*
- Output folder: */Applications/tomcat/webapps/testdrive/ TestDrive-debug*

When you create a new Flex project, Flash Builder creates an MXML file with the same name as the project, as shown in Figure 1-4. This is the main application file where you add your code. You create Flex applications using two languages: ActionScript and MXML. Typically, you use MXML and Flex components to create application interfaces, and ActionScript and events to program application logic. MXML tags and ActionScript code can reference each other, similar to HTML tags and JavaScript code.

When you compile an application, a SWF file is created. You reference the SWF file in an HTML page, and the Flash Player (available as a browser plug-in or ActiveX control) will download and render the SWF file.

Figure 1-4. Create the TestDrive project

In *TestDrive.mxml*, the first line of code is the XML declaration for the parser. The next line is the `<s:Application>` tag, which defines the Application container that must be the root tag for a Flex application. When the application is compiled, a SWF file, an HTML wrapper page that references the SWF file, and other files are placed in the *bin-debug* folder on your application server so you can browse to the application.

Step 3: Use Design Mode to Add Components and Set Properties

Switch to Design mode and drag out Label, DataGrid, and Button components from the Components view to create the interface shown in Figure 1-5. Use the Properties view to assign component IDs of `empBtn`, `deptBtn`, and `empDg`, and set other properties.

HTML applications are built from document elements such as headings, paragraphs, and tables. Flex applications are built from components such as Buttons, CheckBoxes, and Data-Grids. The Flex 4 framework includes over 70 components, including user interface controls to display content and provide user interaction and containers to manage the layout.

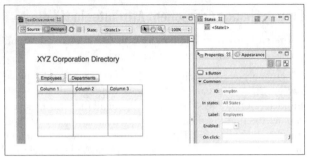

Figure 1-5. Arrange components as shown here

Switch to Source mode and take a look at the generated code. You will see a new tag for each of the components you added. The order of the tags does not matter, because the Application container uses absolute positioning by default, so component positions are set by their *x* and *y* properties.

The `<s:Label>` tag represents a Label control, a very simple user interface component that displays text. Its `text` property is set to `XYZ Corporation Directory`, and its x and y properties are set to the location where it will appear in the interface. The `color` and `fontSize` attributes change the style of the font used. In Flex, you can set color styles to a string for any of the 16 colors in the VGA color set (for example, `red` or `blue`) or an RGB triplet in hexadecimal format (for example, `#FF0000` or `#0000FF`):

```
<s:Label x="36" y="36" text="XYZ
Corporation Directory" color="maroon"
fontSize="20"/>
```

For each component, you can specify properties and styles. Properties apply only to that particular component instance. Styles can be set inline as done here or using CSS to create style rules to apply to your components.

Step 4: Change Component Attributes in MXML

In this step, use the Flash Builder Content Assist to select and set values for various properties and styles.

When you place your cursor inside a tag and press the space bar or Ctrl-space bar, you get code hinting with the Flash Builder Content Assist. It shows a list of all the attributes you can set for that tag, including properties, styles, events, and more (see Figure 1-6). Different symbols represent different attributes. This is the same list you see in the Alphabetical view of the Design mode Properties view.

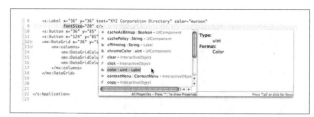

Figure 1-6. Use Content Assist to see a list of all possible tag attributes

You can get more complete descriptions for each of the attributes in the component's API, its application programming interface (Figure 1-7). To navigate to a component's API documentation, select Help→Dynamic Help, then click a component tag in your code. You will see a link to that component's API documentation in the Help view.

Step 5: Browse the Application

Use the Run button or the Run menu to compile the application and view it as an HTML page in a browser window (Figure 1-8).

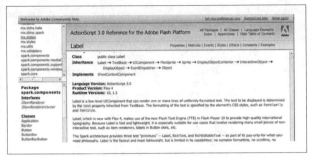

Figure 1-7. View a component's API documentation

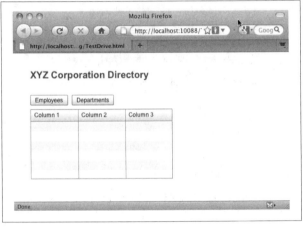

Figure 1-8. View the application in a browser

Your application appears in the browser inside a generated HTML wrapper page. You won't see any data in your application at this point—you should only see the layout. You'll be adding data in Chapter 2. Specifically, you will retrieve and display data in the DataGrid, add application pages, and wire up the buttons.

When you finish this exercise, your code should look like the following:

```xml
<?xml version="1.0" encoding="utf-8"?>
<s:Application xmlns:fx="http://ns.adobe.com/mxml/2009"
               xmlns:s="library://ns.adobe.com/flex/spark"
               xmlns:mx="library://ns.adobe.com/flex/mx"
               minWidth="955" minHeight="600">
    <fx:Declarations>
        <!-- Place non-visual elements
        (e.g., services, value objects) here -->
    </fx:Declarations>
    <s:Label x="36" y="36" text="XYZ Corporation Directory"
        color="maroon" fontSize="20" fontWeight="bold"/>
    <s:Button x="36" y="85" label="Employees" id="empBtn"/>
    <s:Button x="124" y="85" label="Departments"
        id="deptBtn"/>
    <mx:DataGrid x="36" y="114" id="empDg">
        <mx:columns>
            <mx:DataGridColumn headerText="Column 1"
                dataField="col1"/>
            <mx:DataGridColumn headerText="Column 2"
                dataField="col2"/>
            <mx:DataGridColumn headerText="Column 3"
                dataField="col3"/>
        </mx:columns>
    </mx:DataGrid>
</s:Application>
```

Connect to Data

In this section, you will retrieve data from a database and display it in your DataGrid.

This section shows you how to create a data service that uses Flash Remoting to call methods of a PHP class, a ColdFusion component, or a Java class.

Step 1: Create a Flex Data Service

Use the Data menu and the Service Wizard (Connect to Data/ Service) to create a service for your application server. For ColdFusion and Java, specify the service file you put on your application server earlier (see Figure 1-9 for a PHP example). For Java, select the "No password required" checkbox, select the employeeService destination, and change the service package to services.employeeservice.

NOTE

For ColdFusion developers: RDS must be enabled on your server for Flash Builder to create a data service. If you have RDS configured to use a password, you will get an Authentication Required dialog box where you must enter the password or the username and password.

For Java developers: The testdrive application was configured to use RDS with no password. You are changing your generated service package so it matches that used in the solution files, which you can use with PHP, ColdFusion, or J2EE servers.

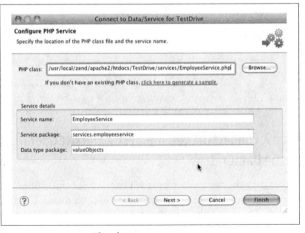

Figure 1-9. Create a Flex data service

Flash Builder introspects the server-side class file and creates a corresponding client-side class with the same operations. You can see your new data service in the Data/Services view (Figure 1-10).

NOTE

For PHP developers: Flash Builder uses the Zend Framework to introspect the service. If this is your first time importing a PHP service, Flash Builder asks you to install the Zend Framework.

For ColdFusion and Java developers: Some of the symbols and data types you see will be different from those shown in Figure 1-10.

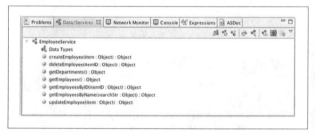

Figure 1-10. Locate your new data service in the Data/Services panel

Step 2: Connect the getEmployees() Service Operation to the DataGrid

Either drag the operation from the Data/Services view onto the DataGrid or select Bind to Data from the Data menu. Configure the return type by autodetecting it from sample data and have it create an array of Employee objects, as shown in Figure 1-11.

Figure 1-11. Specify the return type for the getEmployees() operation

---

NOTE

For Java developers: An array of Employee objects will already be specified as an existing data type.

For PHP and ColdFusion developers: Before Flash Builder can bind the results of the operation to a component, you must specify the action to be taken with the data returned from the operation. You are telling it to create an array of Employee objects, so Flash Builder creates an Employee ActionScript class file with matching properties and uses that. You can also write your PHP classes and ColdFusion component methods to return strongly typed objects instead of general objects.

The DataGrid component has also been updated so that it now has a column for each of the properties contained in the return data objects, as shown in Figure 1-12.

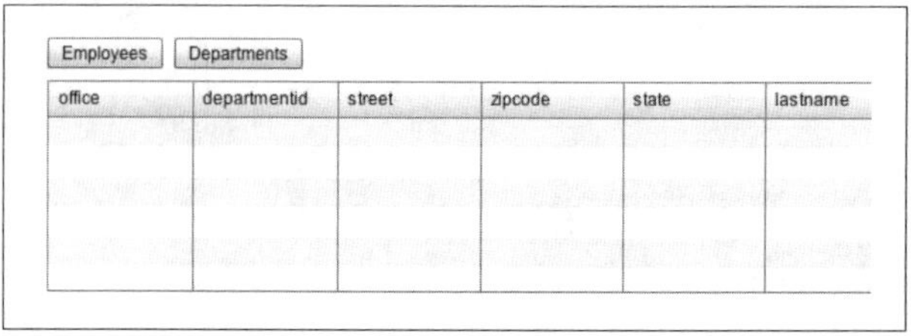

Employees	Departments				
office	departmentid	street	zipcode	state	lastname

Figure 1-12. View the new DataGrid columns

The columns property of the DataGrid object is set equal to an array of DataGridColumn objects where each DataGridColumnObject has properties to specify what data it should display, how big it should be, what its header text should be, and more. The columns will be displayed in the order in which they are defined:

```
<mx:columns>
    <mx:DataGridColumn headerText="office"
        dataField="office"/>
    <mx:DataGridColumn headerText="departmentid"
        dataField="departmentid"/>
    ...
```

Step 3: Look at the Generated Code in Your MXML File

The DataGrid object has a new creationComplete attribute, which specifies that when the creationComplete event occurs, the empDg_creationCompleteHandler() function is called and the event object is passed to it. The DataGrid creationComplete event is broadcast after the DataGrid has been created and all of its properties are set, including its size and position. The event object passed to the function is an instance of the Event class (in this case a FlexEvent) and has properties containing information about the event that occurred:

```
<mx:DataGrid x="36" y="114"
id="empDg"
creationComplete="empDg_creationCompleteHandler(event)"
dataProvider="{getEmployeesResult.lastResult}">
```

An instance of your EmployeeService data service is created inside the Declarations block. You place tags for all nonvisual objects inside the Declaration tag set. The green color of the tag indicates it is a compiler tag associated with compiler instructions and not an instance of a class:

```
<employeeservice:EmployeeService
id="employeeService"
fault="Alert.show(event.fault.faultString + '\n' +
event.fault.faultDetail)" showBusyCursor="true"/>
```

The empDg_creationCompleteHandler() function inside the Script block calls the getEmployees() method of this data service. You place all ActionScript code (which can only include property and method declarations) inside the Script compiler tag:

```
protected function
empDg_creationCompleteHandler(event:FlexEvent):void
{
 getEmployeesResult.token = employeeService.getEmployees();
}
```

When this code is executed, Flash Player makes a call to the server. This happens asynchronously in the background; the user can still interact with the application.

When you make a service call, you need to specify what Flash Player should do when it gets a result or error back from the server. You specified a fault handler for the data service itself, and it will display errors returned from calls to any of its operations in a pop-up box, an instance of the Alert component:

```
<employeeservice:EmployeeService
  id="employeeService"
  fault="Alert.show(event.fault.faultString
  + '\n' + event.fault.faultDetail)"
  showBusyCursor="true"/>
```

A `CallResponder` object handles successful results:

```
<s:CallResponder id="getEmployeesResult"/>
```

This object has a `lastResult` property, which is automatically populated with the data when it is returned to Flash Player from the server. Now you need to associate it with the service call.

When a service call is initiated, an instance of the `AsyncToken` class is created. To associate the `CallResponder` object with the service call, set the `CallResponder`'s `token` property equal to `AsyncToken` generated at the time the service call is made. Now when data is returned from the server, the `CallResponder` object handles it. In addition to getting its `lastResult` property set, `CallResponder` also has `result` and `fault` events for which you can set handlers:

```
getEmployeesResult.token = employeeService.getEmployees();
```

Finally, the `dataProvider` property of the DataGrid is bound to the `lastResult` property of the `CallResponder` object. This means that whenever the value of `getEmployeesResult.lastResult` changes at runtime, the DataGrid's `dataProvider` property is updated and the DataGrid will repopulate itself with the new data:

```
<mx:DataGrid x="36" y="114" id="empDg"
  creationComplete="empDg_creationCompleteHandler(event)"
  dataProvider="{getEmployeesResult.lastResult}">
```

Step 4: Configure DataGrid Columns and Run the Application

Select the DataGrid component in Design mode, click the Configure Columns button in the Properties view, and use the wizard (shown in Figure 1-13) to get the DataGrid to appear as shown in Figure 1-14.

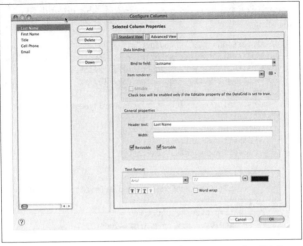

Figure 1-13. Customize the DataGrid layout using the Configure Columns wizard

XYZ Corporation Directory

Employees | Departments

Last Name	First Name	Title	Cell Phone	Email
Smith	Bob	User Research Specialist	(415)444-2222	bsmith@adobe.com
Doe	John	Senior Computer Scientist	(408)444-1111	jdoe@adobe.com
Smith	John	Senior Experience Designer	(408)234-3453	jsmith@adobe.com
Riley	Jane	Quality Engineer	(415)123-4567	jriley@adobe.com
Dent	Arthur	Hitchhiker	(415)324-9870	adent@adobe.com
Chizen	Bruce	Chief Executive Officer	(408)324-3464	bchizen@adobe.com

Figure 1-14. Customize the DataGrid to appear as shown here

When you run the application, you should now see data from the database displayed in the DataGrid. Be sure to sort the data and resize and reorder the columns. You can change the width of an individual column using the Configure Columns button.

When you finish this exercise, your code should look like the following:

```
<?xml version="1.0" encoding="utf-8"?>
<s:Application xmlns:fx="http://ns.adobe.com/mxml/2009"
  xmlns:s="library://ns.adobe.com/flex/spark"
  xmlns:mx="library://ns.adobe.com/flex/mx"
  minWidth="955" minHeight="600"
  xmlns:employeeservice="services.employeeservice.*">
  <fx:Script>
    <![CDATA[
      import mx.controls.Alert;
      import mx.events.FlexEvent;

      protected function
        empDg_creationCompleteHandler(event:FlexEvent):void
      {
        getEmployeesResult.token =
          employeeService.getEmployees();
      }
    ]]>
  </fx:Script>
  <fx:Declarations>
    <s:CallResponder id="getEmployeesResult" />
    <employeeservice:EmployeeService id="employeeService"
      fault="Alert.show(event.fault.faultString + '\n' +
      event.fault.faultDetail)"
      showBusyCursor="true"/>
  </fx:Declarations>

  <s:Label x="36" y="36" text="XYZ Corporation Directory"
    color="maroon" fontSize="20" fontWeight="bold"/>
  <s:Button x="36" y="85" label="Employees" id="empBtn"/>
  <s:Button x="124" y="85" label="Departments"
    id="deptBtn"/>
  <mx:DataGrid x="36" y="114" id="empDg"
    creationComplete="empDg_creationCompleteHandler(event)"
    dataProvider="{getEmployeesResult.lastResult}"
    width="650">
    <mx:columns>
      <mx:DataGridColumn headerText="Last Name"
        dataField="lastname"/>
      <mx:DataGridColumn headerText="First Name"
        dataField="firstname"/>
      <mx:DataGridColumn headerText="Title"
        dataField="title" width="170"/>
      <mx:DataGridColumn headerText="Cell Phone"
```

```
            dataField="cellphone"/>
        <mx:DataGridColumn headerText="Email"
            dataField="email" width="130"/>
    </mx:columns>
  </mx:DataGrid>
</s:Application>
```

This application contains a single page that displays a list of employees. In the next section, you will create additional "pages" to view employee details and a list of departments.

Create Pages

In this section, you will create different pages in your application. HTML applications use pages as screens, but in Flex, you use a related but different concept called *states*. As you'll see, unlike HTML, states do not necessarily appear in separate files.

You are going to create three states. The first is the interface you already built that appears when the application starts. The other two states will be Departments and EmployeeDetails, which will appear when a user clicks the Departments button or selects a row in the DataGrid, respectively.

Step 1: Create Employees and Departments States

In Design mode, use the States view to create a new state called Departments based on the existing state, <State1>. In Departments, delete the existing DataGrid and add a new DataGrid called deptDg and a Button, as shown in Figure 1-15. Rename <State1> to Employees (Figure 1-16).

Unlike in HTML pages, in Flex applications the same component can be part of more than one state. The XYZ Label and the Employees and Departments buttons are included in both the Employees and Departments states.

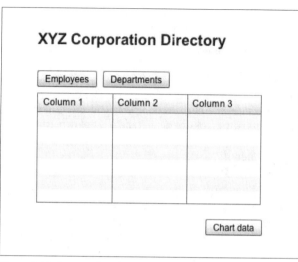

Figure 1-15. Lay out the Departments state

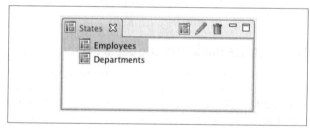

Figure 1-16. Create the Employees and Departments states

Take a look at the generated code. You will see the two states defined; the Application **states** property is set equal to an array of State objects for which you assign names:

```
<s:states>
    <s:State name="Employees"/>
    <s:State name="Departments"/>
</s:states>
```

The first DataGrid now has a property, includeIn, set to Employees, the only state for which it should be displayed:

```
<mx:DataGrid x="36" y="114" id="empDg"
   creationComplete="empDg_creationCompleteHandler(event)"
   dataProvider="{getEmployeesResult.lastResult}"
   width="650" includeIn="Employees">
```

The second DataGrid and the new Button are only included in the Departments state. Components without an includeIn property (or an excludeFrom property) are included in all states. You can specify multiple states using a comma-delimited list.

Step 2: Retrieve and Display Department Data in the Departments DataGrid

Bind the Departments DataGrid to the getDepartments() service operation and configure the return type to be an array of new Department objects. Use the Configure Columns wizard to customize the DataGrid (shown in Figure 1-17).

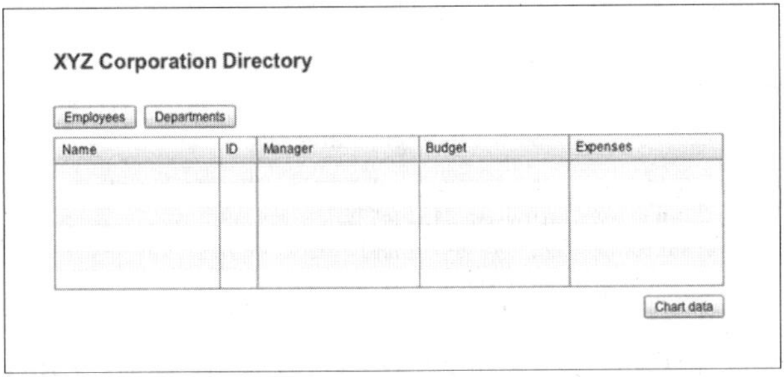

Figure 1-17. Configure the Departments DataGrid

Take a look at the generated code. All the code should look familiar.

Step 3: Change Property Values in Different States

In Design mode, set the Employees Button's enabled property to false in the Employees state and the Departments Button's enabled property to false in the Departments state (Figure 1-18).

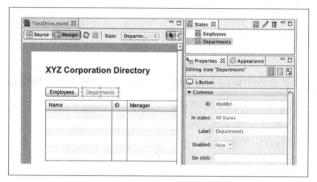

Figure 1-18. Disable the Departments button in the Departments state

Switch to Source mode. The enabled property of each Button has been set to false for a single state:

```
<s:Button x="36" y="85" label="Employees" id="empBtn"
    enabled.Employees="false"/>
<s:Button x="124" y="85" label="Departments" id="deptBtn"
    enabled.Departments="false"/>
```

Step 4: Change a Property or Style Value in All States

In Design mode, change the color of the Label and then, in the States panel, select the other state; the color is changed for only the selected state. Apply the new color to all states by selecting Apply Current Properties to All States from the Label's context menu (shown in Figure 1-19).

When you first set the color in Design mode, some state is selected so you get the code color.somestate=somevalue. When you select to apply current properties to all states, this becomes color=somevalue instead and will be the value for all of the states that you have specified to include this component in.

Step 5: Create a New EmployeeDetails State

Base the new state on the Employees state. From the Data-Grid's context menu in the new state, select Generate Details Form. Using the wizard (Figure 1-20), create a noneditable form that does not make a detail call. Arrange the layout as shown in Figure 1-21 by dragging out a second Form container from the Layout section of the Components view and dragging FormItem controls from one Form container to another.

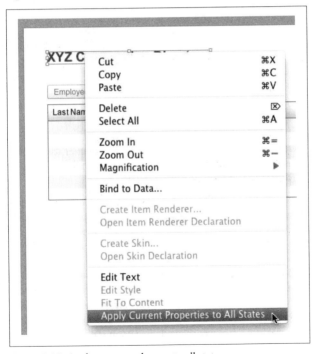

Figure 1-19. Apply property changes to all states

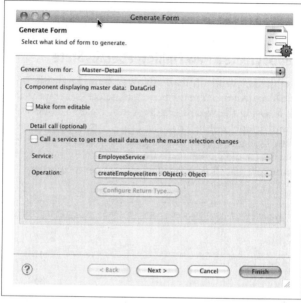

Figure 1-20. Generate a Master-Detail form

In Flex applications, a Form is simply a container that makes it easier to align your controls. Unlike HTML, it does not group data for submitting data to the server.

Here, you are not making a service call to retrieve the details for a specific employee, because you already have all the details for every employee on the client. When getEmployees() is initially called to populate the DataGrid, all the employee data is retrieved. Thus, you only need to show the data for the selected employee in the form. If you have lots of records with lots of fields, you initially may want to retrieve only the properties of the employees you are going to display in the grid and then make a service call to getEmployeesByID() to retrieve all the data for a specific employee to be displayed in the form.

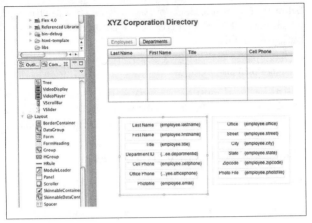

Figure 1-21. Lay out the EmployeeDetails state

Rename the labels for the Form fields and rearrange the FormItem components as shown in Figure 1-21 by dragging and dropping them to different locations in the Form containers.

Switch to Source mode and look at the generated code. You will see your new EmployeeDetails state defined in the states tag and you will see two new Form tags. Notice that the text property of all the Label controls in the FormItem tags are bound to a property of an employee object:

```
<mx:Form includeIn="EmployeeDetails" x="63" y="325">
    <mx:FormItem label="Last Name">
        <s:Label id="lastnameLabel"
                 text="{employee.lastname}"/>
    </mx:FormItem>
```

Look in the Declarations section. You will see the employee object defined as an instance of the Employee class:

```
<valueObjects:Employee id="employee"/>
```

Below the `Declarations` section, you will see a new `Binding` tag, which binds the `selectedItem` of the `empDg` DataGrid to this `employee` variable:

```
<fx:Binding source="empDg.selectedItem as Employee"
  destination="employee"/>
```

The `as` keyword must be used to cast the selectedItem to an Employee because the `selectedItem` property is defined as a general object, but the employee must be an Employee object.

Step 6: Add Objects to Specific States

Add four buttons (`updateBtn`, `deleteBtn`, `addBtn`, `searchBtn`) and a TextInput (`searchTxt`) to the EmployeeDetails state (see Figure 1-22). Give the TextInput an initial value of "Enter last name here..." Switch to the Employees state; you will not see the new components. Return to the EmployeeDetails state, select the Add Button and, in the Property view, include the Button in the Employees state (see Figure 1-23). Repeat for `searchTxt` and `searchBtn` and run the application, shown in Figure 1-24.

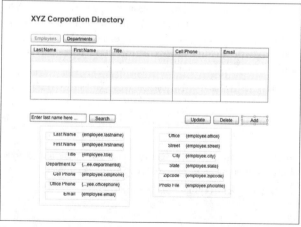

Figure 1-22. Add new components to EmployeeDetails

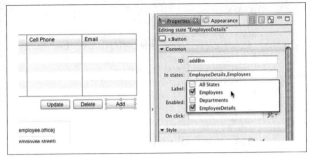

Figure 1-23. Specify which states should include an object

XYZ Corporation Directory

Employees | Departments

Last Name	First Name	Title	Cell Phone	Email
Smith	Bob	User Research Specialist	(415)444-2222	bsmith@adobe.com
Doe	John	Senior Computer Scientist	(408)444-1111	jdoe@adobe.com
Smith	John	Senior Experience Designer	(408)234-3453	jsmith@adobe.com
Riley	Jane	Quality Engineer	(415)123-4567	jriley@adobe.com
Dent	Arthur	Hitchhiker	(415)324-9870	adent@adobe.com
Chizen	Bruce	Chief Executive Officer	(408)324-3464	bchizen@adobe.com

Enter last name here ... | Search | | Add

Figure 1-24. Run the application; you will see only the Employees state

You have now created three states representing pages in your
application. You will write event handlers to switch between
the states, populate the details form, and search the employees
in Chapter 2. You will also wire up the Update, Delete, and
Add Buttons in Chapter 2.

Your code will look like the following at the end of this step
(you can download the complete sample code at
*www.adobe.com/devnet/flex/testdrive/assets/test
drive_build_app.zip*):

```
<?xml version="1.0" encoding="utf-8"?>
<s:Application xmlns:valueObjects="valueObjects.*" ...>
  <fx:Script>
```

```
    <![CDATA[
      (...)
      protected function
       deptDg_creationCompleteHandler(event:FlexEvent):void
      {
        getDepartmentsResult.token =
          employeeService.getDepartments();
      }
      ]]>
  </fx:Script>
  <s:states>
    <s:State name="Employees"/>
    <s:State name="Departments"/>
    <s:State name="EmployeeDetails"/>
  </s:states>
  <fx:Declarations>
    (...)
    <s:CallResponder id="getEmployeesResult"/>
    <valueObjects:Employee id="employee"/>
  </fx:Declarations>
  <fx:Binding source="empDg.selectedItem as Employee"
    destination="employee"/>

  <s:Label text="XYZ Corporation Directory"
    color="#1239E3" .../>
  <s:Button id="empBtn" enabled.Employees="false"
    enabled.EmployeeDetails="false" .../>
  <s:Button id="deptBtn" enabled.Departments="false" .../>
  <mx:DataGrid id="empDg"
    includeIn="EmployeeDetails,Employees" .../>
  <mx:DataGrid includeIn="Departments" x="36" y="114"
    id="deptDg"
    creationComplete=
      "deptDg_creationCompleteHandler(event)"
    dataProvider="{getDepartmentsResult.lastResult}"
    width="650" height="152">
    <mx:columns>
        <mx:DataGridColumn headerText="Name"
          dataField="name" width="170"/>
        <mx:DataGridColumn headerText="ID"
          dataField="id" width="40"/>
        <mx:DataGridColumn headerText="Manager"
          dataField="manager" width="170"/>
        <mx:DataGridColumn dataField="budget"
          headerText="Budget" width="155"/>
        <mx:DataGridColumn dataField="actualexpenses"
          headerText="Expenses" width="155"/>
```

```
      </mx:columns>
   </mx:DataGrid>
   <s:Button includeIn="Departments" x="609" y="293"
     label="Chart data"/>
   <mx:Form includeIn="EmployeeDetails" x="36" y="325">
      <mx:FormItem label="Last Name">
         <s:Label id="lastnameLabel"
           text="{employee.lastname}"/>
      </mx:FormItem>
      <mx:FormItem label="First Name">
         <s:Label id="firstnameLabel"
           text="{employee.firstname}"/>
      </mx:FormItem>
      <mx:FormItem label="Title">
         <s:Label id="titleLabel"
           text="{employee.title}"/>
      </mx:FormItem>
      <mx:FormItem label="Department ID">
         <s:Label id="departmentidLabel"
           text="{employee.departmentid}"/>
      </mx:FormItem>
      <mx:FormItem label="Cell Phone">
         <s:Label id="cellphoneLabel"
           text="{employee.cellphone}"/>
      </mx:FormItem>
      <mx:FormItem label="Office Phone">
         <s:Label id="officephoneLabel"
           text="{employee.officephone}"/>
      </mx:FormItem>
      <mx:FormItem label="Email">
         <s:Label id="emailLabel"
           text="{employee.email}"/>
      </mx:FormItem>
   </mx:Form>
   <mx:Form includeIn="EmployeeDetails" x="308" y="325">
      <mx:FormItem label="Office">
         <s:Label id="officeLabel"
           text="{employee.office}"/>
      </mx:FormItem>
      <mx:FormItem label="Street">
         <s:Label id="streetLabel"
           text="{employee.street}"/>
      </mx:FormItem>
      <mx:FormItem label="City">
         <s:Label id="cityLabel"
           text="{employee.city}"/>
      </mx:FormItem>
```

```
            <mx:FormItem label="State">
                <s:Label id="stateLabel"
                    text="{employee.state}"/>
            </mx:FormItem>
            <mx:FormItem label="Zipcode">
                <s:Label id="zipcodeLabel"
                    text="{employee.zipcode}"/>
            </mx:FormItem>
            <mx:FormItem label="Photo File">
                <s:Label id="photofileLabel"
                    text="{employee.photofile}"/>
            </mx:FormItem>
        </mx:Form>
        <s:Button includeIn="EmployeeDetails" x="459" y="293"
            label="Update" id="updateBtn"/>
        <s:Button includeIn="EmployeeDetails,Employees"
            label="Add " id="addBtn" x="615" y="293"/>
        <s:Button includeIn="EmployeeDetails" x="537" y="293"
            label="Delete " id="deleteBtn"/>
        <s:TextInput includeIn="EmployeeDetails,Employees"
            text="Enter last name here ..." width="153"
            id="searchTxt" x="36" y="292"/>
        <s:Button includeIn="EmployeeDetails,Employees"
            label="Search" id="searchBtn" x="197" y="293"/>
    </s:Application>
```

Code Your Interactions

In Flex, when a user interacts with a component, it broadcasts
events such as click, rollOver, or rollOut events. To respond
to an event, you specify an event handler function to be called
when that event occurs.

In this section, you will write event handlers to switch between
the application states when users click buttons, populate the
details form when users select DataGrid rows, and search the
employees when users click buttons.

Step 1: Generate an Event Handler

In Design view, right-click the Departments button and select
Generate Click Handler. Make this the click handler for all
states.

Flash Builder automatically switches to Source mode, and you will see the following new function:

```
protected function
  deptBtn_clickHandler(event:MouseEvent):void
{
// TODO Auto-generated method stub
}
```

You will also see the following `click` event attribute in the Departments `Button` tag:

```
<s:Button x="124" y="85" label="Departments"
  id="deptBtn" enabled.Departments="false"
  click.EmployeeDetails="deptBtn_clickHandler(event)"/>
```

When the user clicks this button in the EmployeeDetails state, that event handler function will be called. Change the `click` event attribute in the Departments `Button` tag so that the following represents the `click` handler for all states:

```
<s:Button x="124" y="85"
  label="Departments" id="deptBtn"
  enabled.Departments="false"
  click ="deptBtn_clickHandler(event)"/>
```

Step 2: Change to the Departments State on a Button click Event

Inside the function, switch to the Departments state by setting the `currentState` property of the Application to Departments. Run the application.

The Departments Button `click` event handler should appear like the following:

```
protected function
  deptBtn_clickHandler(event:MouseEvent):void
{
  currentState="Departments";
}
```

When you run the application, you should be able to click the Departments button to switch to the Departments state (shown in Figure 1-25). Notice that the Employees button is now enabled and the Departments button is disabled.

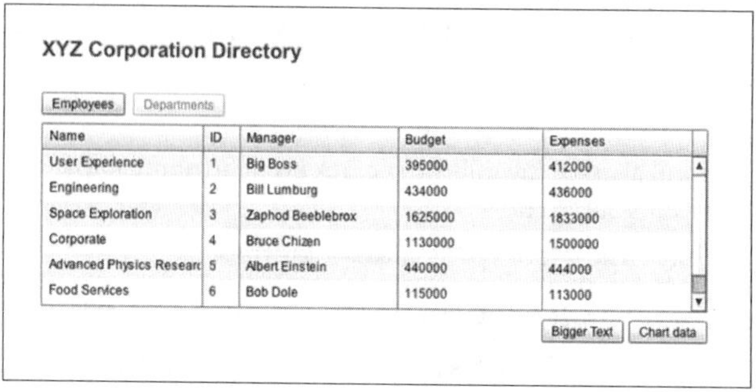

Figure 1-25. *In a browser, switch to the Departments state*

Step 3: Change to the Employees State on a Button click Event

With the Departments state selected in Design mode, generate an event handler for the Employees button and, inside the function, switch to the Employees state.

The Employees button click event handler should appear like the following:

```
protected function
  empBtn_clickHandler(event:MouseEvent):void
{
  currentState = "Employees";
}
```

In the Employees Button tag, you can leave the attribute as click.Departments or change it to click. Both will work because this button is only enabled and clickable in the Departments state.

When you run the application, you should now be able to switch back and forth between the Departments and Employees states. When you select a row in the employee DataGrid, nothing happens.

Step 4: Change to the EmployeeDetails State on a DataGrid change Event

In Source mode, add a change attribute to the empDg DataGrid and generate a change handler (see Figure 1-26). Inside the handler, set currentState to EmployeeDetails.

Figure 1-26. Generate a DataGrid change event handler

The DataGrid change event handler should appear as follows:

```
protected function
  empDg_changeHandler(event:ListEvent):void

{
  currentState="EmployeeDetails";
}
```

Now when you run the application, you should be able to select a row in the employee DataGrid and see the details for that employee, as shown in Figure 1-27.

Step 5: Clear the TextInput Component on a focusIn Event

In Design mode, select the TextInput component and click the lightning bolt next to the focusIn event in the Events section of the Properties Category view (see Figure 1-28). Inside the generated handler, clear the text field.

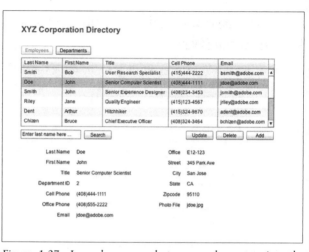

Figure 1-27. In a browser, select an employee to view the EmployeeDetails state

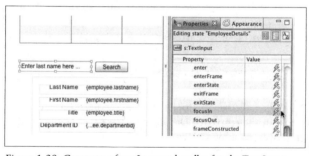

Figure 1-28. Generate a focusIn event handler for the TextInput

Enter the following code inside your focusIn event handler, making sure the initial value of the search string you specify here exactly matches the value you specified in the TextInput tag:

```
protected function
  searchTxt_focusInHandler(event:FocusEvent):void
  {
```

```
    if(searchTxt.text=="Enter last name here ...")
      searchTxt.text="";
}
```

In your TextInput tag, remove the state associated with the
focusIn event so it appears as shown here:

```
<s:TextInput includeIn="EmployeeDetails,Employees"
   text="Enter last name here ..." width="153"
   id="searchTxt" x="36" y="292"
   focusIn="searchTxt_focusInHandler(event)"/>
```

Run the application. When you click in the TextInput component, the initial help text should disappear.

Step 6: Load New Data on a click Event

Using the Data/Services view, configure the getEmployeesBy
Name() operation to return an array of existing Employee objects; enter a parameter value of Smith when autodetecting from
sample data. Drag the getEmployeesByName() operation onto
the Search button. Inside the generated event handler, pass the
user-entered value, which is held in searchTxt.text, to the
operation. Change the responder to be the existing
getEmployeesResult responder. Apply the searchBtn click
event to all states.

By default, the following new responder, getEmployeesBy
NameResult, is created:

```
<s:CallResponder id="getEmployeesByNameResult"/>
```

This responder is used for the following service call:

```
protected function
  searchBtn_clickHandler(event:MouseEvent):void
{
  getEmployeesByNameResult.token =
    employeeService.getEmployeesByName(searchTxt.text);
}
```

You want the results to be displayed in the existing empDg DataGrid, though, so change the responder to be the existing
getEmployeesResult responder whose lastResult property is
already bound to the dataProvider of the DataGrid, as follows:

```
protected function
  searchBtn_clickHandler(event:MouseEvent):void
{
  getEmployeesResult.token =
    employeeService.getEmployeesByName(searchTxt.text);
}
```

You are not using the generated getEmployeesByNameResult responder, so you can delete its definition, shown here:

```
<s:CallResponder id="getEmployeesByNameResult"/>
```

Run the application and enter a last name like "Smith" in the search field, then click Search. A new service call is made to the server and the responder is populated with this new data, so the data displayed in the DataGrid changes.

In this exercise, you are calling a method on the server to perform the employee filtering. However, because you already returned all the employee records to the client, you can filter the records locally instead. This is more efficient, because it avoids unnecessary calls to the server.

Step 7: Use Conditional Logic to Retrieve All or Only Some Records

Modify the searchBtn click handler so that it calls getEmployeesByName() if searchTxt.text has a value, and getEmployees() if it does not.

Your event handler should appear as follows:

```
protected function
  searchBtn_clickHandler(event:MouseEvent):void
{
  if(searchTxt.text!=""){
    getEmployeesResult.token =
      employeeService.getEmployeesByName(searchTxt.text);
  }
  else{
    getEmployeesResult.token =
      employeeService.getEmployees();
  }
}
```

Run the application. Search by a name and view the results. Next, remove any search string and search. You should see all the employees listed again.

Step 8: Modify Object Styles on a click Event

Add a new Button control, `biggerBtn`, to the Departments view (see Figure 1-29). Generate a `click` handler for it that uses the `setStyle()` method to increase the DataGrid `fontSize` style.

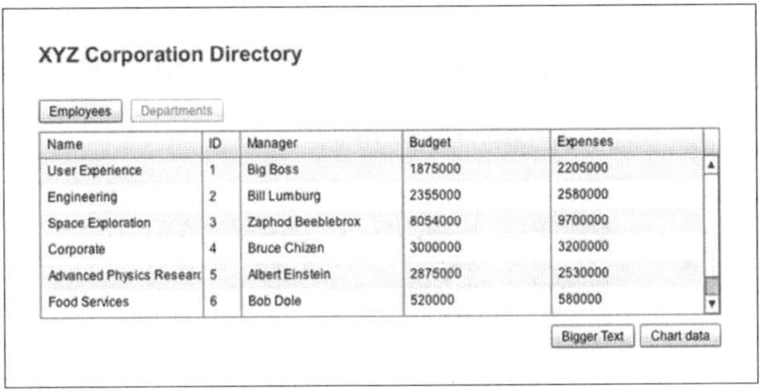

XYZ Corporation Directory

`Employees` `Departments`

Name	ID	Manager	Budget	Expenses
User Experience	1	Big Boss	1875000	2205000
Engineering	2	Bill Lumburg	2355000	2580000
Space Exploration	3	Zaphod Beeblebrox	8054000	9700000
Corporate	4	Bruce Chizen	3000000	3200000
Advanced Physics Research	5	Albert Einstein	2875000	2530000
Food Services	6	Bob Dole	520000	580000

`Bigger Text` `Chart data`

Figure 1-29. Add a Bigger Text button to the Departments view

The `click` handler should appear as follows:

```
protected function
  biggerBtn_clickHandler(event:MouseEvent):void
{
  deptDg.setStyle("fontSize",14);
}
```

You cannot change styles at runtime using the `object.property=value` notation you use to set properties. Instead, you have to use the `setStyle()` method. You can set and apply properties to only one instance of an object, whereas you can set styles in multiple places (inline, in CSS, or inherited), so setting a style on one object may also change the style of other objects. Use a `StyleManager` class to manage all the styles.

Run the application, switch to Departments, and click the Bigger Text button. The text in the DataGrid should get bigger.

When you finish coding your interactions, your code should look like the following (you can download the complete sample code at *www.adobe.com/devnet/flex/testdrive/assets/test drive_build_app.zip*):

```
<?xml version="1.0" encoding="utf-8"?>
<s:Application ...>
  <fx:Script>
    <![CDATA[
      (...)
      import mx.events.ListEvent;

      protected function
        deptBtn_clickHandler(event:MouseEvent):void
      {
        currentState="Departments";
      }
      protected function
        empBtn_clickHandler(event:MouseEvent):void
      {
        currentState="Employees";
      }
      protected function
        empDg_changeHandler(event:ListEvent):void
      {
        currentState="EmployeeDetails";
      }
      protected function
        searchTxt_focusInHandler(event:FocusEvent):void
      {
        if(searchTxt.text=="Enter last name here ... ")
          searchTxt.text="";
      }
      protected function
        searchBtn_clickHandler(event:MouseEvent):void
      {
        if(searchTxt.text!=""){
        getEmployeesResult.token =
          employeeService.getEmployeesByName(
          searchTxt.text);
        }
        else{
          getEmployeesResult.token =
          employeeService.getEmployees();
        }
      }
```

```
    protected function
      biggerBtn_clickHandler(event:MouseEvent):void
    {
      deptDg.setStyle("fontSize",16);
    }
  ]]>
</fx:Script>
(...)
<s:Button id="empBtn"
  click.Departments="empBtn_clickHandler(event)" .../>
<s:Button id="deptBtn"
  click="deptBtn_clickHandler(event)" .../>
<mx:DataGrid id="empDg"
  change="empDg_changeHandler(event)" .../>
(...)
<s:TextInput id="SearchTxt"
  focusIn="searchTxt_focusInHandler(event)" .../>
<s:Button id="searchBtn"
  click="searchBtn_clickHandler(event)" .../>
<s:Button id="biggerBtn"
  click="biggerBtn_clickHandler(event)" .../>
</s:Application>
```

Congratulations! In about an hour, you've built a Flex application with multiple states that can load and display data and perform database queries.

To build on your knowledge, see Chapter 2 to learn about updating your database based on user input, Chapters 3 and 4 to learn about debugging and deploying your application, and Chapters 5 and 6 to learn about customizing the application appearance and using the expressive Flex charting components.

Modify the Database

In Chapter 1, you retrieved data from a database and displayed it. In this chapter, you will write your Flex application to perform your data CRUD, that is, to create, read, update, and delete data from the database.

Add Data Using a Form

In this section, you will create a new EmployeeAdd state that has an input form for users to add a new employee to the database.

Step 1: Create a New EmployeeAdd State

Create a new EmployeeAdd state based on the EmployeeDetails state. In the new state, delete the two forms and disable the Add, Delete, and Update Buttons (Figure 2-1).

Step 2: Create an Input Form

From the DataGrid context menu, select Generate Details Form. In the wizard, make the form editable, do not make a detail service call, and click Next. In the Property Control Mapping, choose not to display the **id**, and arrange the fields in the order in which you want them displayed (see Figure 2-2).

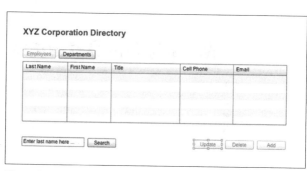

Figure 2-1. Create a new EmployeeAdd state

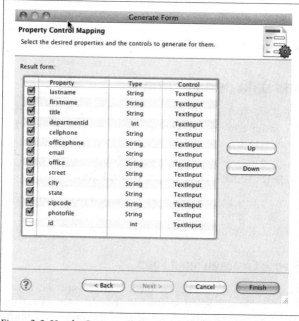

Figure 2-2. Use the Generate Form wizard to create an editable Details form

Switch to Source mode and look at the generated code. You will see similar code to that generated in Chapter 1 for the EmployeeDetails state. You will see your new EmployeeAdd state defined in the states tag and a new Form tag. In this case, though, the FormItem tags contain TextInput controls instead of Label controls.

Notice that the text properties of all the TextInput controls in the FormItem tags are bound to a property of an employee2 object:

```
<mx:Form includeIn="EmployeeAdd" defaultButton="{button}">
    <mx:FormItem label="lastname">
        <s:TextInput id=" lastnameTextInput"
            text="{employee2.lastname}"/>
    </mx:FormItem>
```

Look in the Declarations section. You will see the employee2 object defined as an instance of the Employee class, as follows:

```
<valueObjects:Employee id="employee2"/>
```

Below the Declarations section, you will see a new Binding tag, which binds the selectedItem of the empDg DataGrid to this employee2 variable, as follows:

```
<fx:Binding source="empDg.selectedItem as Employee"
    destination="employee2"/>
```

All this code is redundant; employee is equal to employee2, and the variables are referencing the same object in memory. The Generate Form wizard does not allow you to specify an existing object to display (in this case, employee), so it generates and binds to a new variable, employee2.

Locate the new Button at the end of the new Form. It has the following click event handler already defined:

```
<s:Button id="button" label="Submit"
    click="button_clickHandler(event)"/>
```

Locate the corresponding handler in the **Script** block. It sets the properties of the **employee2** object equal to the new values entered by the user in the TextInput form fields:

```
protected function
  button_clickHandler(event:MouseEvent):void
{
  employee2.lastname = lastnameTextInput.text;
  employee2.firstname = firstnameTextInput.text;
  employee2.title = titleTextInput.text;
  employee2.departmentid =
    parseInt(departmentidTextInput.text);
  employee2.cellphone = cellphoneTextInput.text;
  employee2.officephone = officephoneTextInput.text;
  employee2.email = emailTextInput.text;
  employee2.office = officeTextInput.text;
  employee2.street = streetTextInput.text;
  employee2.city = cityTextInput.text;
  employee2.state = stateTextInput.text;
  employee2.zipcode = zipcodeTextInput.text;
  employee2.photofile = photofileTextInput.text;
}
```

Step 3: Use the employee Object Instead of employee2

Delete the binding and declaration tags for **employee2** and change the references to **employee2** in the new Form and in the **button_clickHandler()** to **employee**.

Delete the following lines of code:

```
<fx:Binding source="empDg.selectedItem as Employee"
  destination="employee2"/>
<valueObjects:Employee id="employee2"/>
```

All the TextInput controls in the new Form should look similar to the following:

```
<mx:FormItem label="Last Name">
  <s:TextInput id="lastnameTextInput"
    text="{employee.lastname}"/>
</mx:FormItem>
```

And all the statements in the **button_clickHandler()** function should look similar to the following:

```
employee.lastname = lastnameTextInput.text;
```

Step 4: Modify the Form Layout

Arrange the input form as shown in Figure 2-3 by dragging out a second Form container from the Layout section of the Components view and dragging FormItems from one Form container to another. Edit the `label` properties and change the Submit Button `label` to Add.

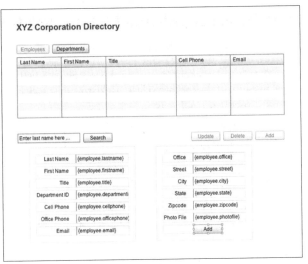

Figure 2-3. Lay out the EmployeeAdd state as shown here

Here are some tips for arranging your forms:

- You can use Shift+click to select multiple items and move them all from one Form container to the other.
- Look at the *x* and *y* positions of the two forms in the EmployeeDetails state and use these for the positions of the new forms so they appear in exactly the same places.

- To align the Add button with the form fields above it, place it inside of a FormItem with no `label` property set, as follows:

```
<mx:FormItem>
  <s:Button id="button" label="Add"
    click="button_clickHandler(event)"/>
</mx:FormItem>
```

Step 5: Switch States When the Add Button Is Clicked

Generate a `click` handler for the Add button above the form (not the one in the form) and inside the handler, set the `currentState` to `EmployeeAdd`, and set the `employee` variable to a new instance of the `Employee` class. Make this the `click` handler for this Button in all states.

Your event handler should appear as follows:

```
protected function
  addBtn_clickHandler(event:MouseEvent):void
{
  currentState="EmployeeAdd";
  employee=new Employee();
}
```

Change the `addBtn` Button control so that it is the `click` handler for all states, as follows:

```
<s:Button includeIn="EmployeeAdd,EmployeeDetails,Employees"
  label="Add" id="addBtn" x="615" y="293"
  enabled.EmployeeAdd="false"
  click="addBtn_clickHandler(event)"/>
```

Run the application and click the Add button. You should see a blank input form similar to the one shown in Figure 2-4.

Step 6: Submit Data to the Server

Drag the `createEmployee()` operation from the Data/Services panel and drop it on the Add button in the Form. In the generated handler, pass `employee` to the service operation.

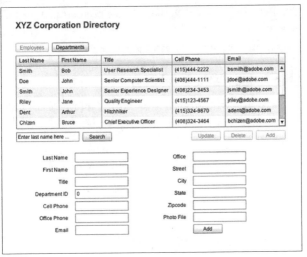

Figure 2-4. In a browser, view the new EmployeeAdd state

Your handler should appear as follows:

```
protected function
  button_clickHandler(event:MouseEvent):void
{
  employee.lastname = lastnameTextInput.text;
  employee.firstname = firstnameTextInput.text;
  employee.title = titleTextInput.text;
  employee.departmentid =
    parseInt(departmentidTextInput.text);
  employee.cellphone = cellphoneTextInput.text;
  employee.officephone = officephoneTextInput.text;
  employee.email = emailTextInput.text;
  employee.office = officeTextInput.text;
  employee.street = streetTextInput.text;
  employee.city = cityTextInput.text;
  employee.state = stateTextInput.text;
  employee.zipcode = zipcodeTextInput.text;
  employee.photofile = photofileTextInput.text;
  createEmployeeResult.token =
    employeeService.createEmployee(employee);
}
```

The following new CallResponder has been created for this service call:

```
<s:CallResponder id="createEmployeeResult"/>
```

Step 7: Update the Local Data

Add a `result` event attribute to the `createEmployeeResult` Call-Responder and generate an event handler (see Figure 2-5). Inside the handler, set `currentState` to EmployeeDetails, set the `id` for the new employee, and use the `addItem()` method to add the new employee to the DataGrid `dataProvider`.

Figure 2-5. Generate a result event handler for the CallResponder

Your `createEmployeeResult` CallResponder should appear as follows:

```
<s:CallResponder id="createEmployeeResult"
  result="createEmployeeResult_resultHandler(event)"/>
```

The `result` event handler should appear as follows:

```
protected function
  createEmployeeResult_resultHandler(
    event:ResultEvent):void
{
  currentState="EmployeeDetails";
  employee.id=event.result as int;
  empDg.dataProvider.addItem(employee);
}
```

After you have successfully added the data to the database, the EmployeeDetails state will be shown with the details for this new employee. At this point, though, the new employee has been saved in the database, but not in the collection of data being displayed in the DataGrid. You need to assign the newly generated `id` to `employee` and add `employee` to the data displayed in the DataGrid.

If you look in the TestDrive server-side service file, you will see that the `createEmployee()` method returns an integer equal to the `id` of the new employee inserted in the database. The data returned from a server-side method call is stored in the `result` property of the `event` object that is passed to the `result` event handler. The `id` property of `employee` is data typed as an integer. The `result` property of the `event` object is data typed as a general object. You have to cast `event.result` to an integer to set `id` equal to it.

NOTE

You will use the Flash Builder debugger to examine the properties of the `event` object and other objects in Chapter 3.

`addItem()` is a method of the Flex `ArrayCollection` class. When the employee data is initially retrieved from the server, it stores the data as an ArrayCollection of Employee objects as the DataGrid `dataProvider`.

NOTE

In this example, you are writing code to update both the server-side data (stored in the database) and the client-side data (stored in the DataGrid `dataProvider`). Flash Builder also has a data management feature you can use to help synchronize client- and server-side data.

Run the application and add a new employee. You did not make any of the fields required, but enter at least a last name so you can easily find your new record. You will have to scroll in the DataGrid to see your new record.

Refresh the browser and make sure you see your new employee in the DataGrid.

Step 8: Select and Show the New Record in the DataGrid

Inside the `createEmployeeResult` result handler, set the Data-Grid `selectedItem` to `employee`, set the DataGrid `vertical ScrollPosition` to the DataGrid control's `selectedIndex`, and use the `validateNow()` method to force the DataGrid to update its display.

Your `result` event handler should appear as follows:

```
protected function
  createEmployeeResult_resultHandler(
    event:ResultEvent):void
{
  currentState="EmployeeDetails";
  employee.id=event.result as int;
  empDg.dataProvider.addItem(employee);
  empDg.selectedItem =employee;
  empDg.verticalScrollPosition=empDg.selectedIndex;
  empDg.validateNow();
}
```

For performance reasons, the DataGrid sometimes defers updating its display. The `validateNow()` method forces it to update its display. Although appropriate here, be careful using `validateNow()`, because it can cause performance problems if called too often.

Run the application and add a new employee. The new employee should now be selected and displayed in the DataGrid (Figure 2-6).

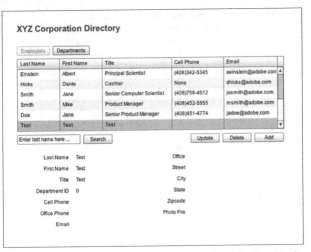

Figure 2-6. The newly added employee is selected and displayed in the
DataGrid

After you've added the new employee, your code should look
like the following (you can download the complete sample
code at *www.adobe.com/devnet/flex/testdrive/assets/test
drive_modify_data.zip*):

```
<?xml version="1.0" encoding="utf-8"?>
<s:Application ...>
  <fx:Script>
    <![CDATA[
      (...)
      import mx.rpc.events.ResultEvent;

      protected function
        button_clickHandler(event:MouseEvent):void
      {
        employee.lastname = lastnameTextInput.text;
        employee.firstname = firstnameTextInput.text;
        employee.title = titleTextInput.text;
        employee.departmentid =
          parseInt(departmentidTextInput.text);
        employee.cellphone = cellphoneTextInput.text;
        employee.officephone =
```

```
                    officephoneTextInput.text;
            employee.email = emailTextInput.text;
            employee.office = officeTextInput.text;
            employee.street = streetTextInput.text;
            employee.city = cityTextInput.text;
            employee.state = stateTextInput.text;
            employee.zipcode = zipcodeTextInput.text;
            employee.photofile = photofileTextInput.text;
            createEmployeeResult.token =
                employeeService.createEmployee(employee);
        }
        protected function
            addBtn_clickHandler(event:MouseEvent):void
        {
            currentState="EmployeeAdd";
            employee=new Employee();
        }
        protected function
            createEmployeeResult_resultHandler(
                event:ResultEvent):void
        {
            currentState="EmployeeDetails";
            employee.id=event.result as int;
            empDg.dataProvider.addItem(employee);
            empDg.selectedItem =employee;
            empDg.verticalScrollPosition=
                empDg.selectedIndex;
            empDg.validateNow();
        }
    ]]>
</fx:Script>
<s:states>
    (...)
    <s:State name="EmployeeAdd"/>
</s:states>
<fx:Declarations>
    (...)

<s:Button id="empBtn" enabled.EmployeeAdd="false" .../>
<mx:DataGrid
    includeIn="EmployeeAdd,EmployeeDetails,Employees" .../>
<s:Button id="updateBtn"
    includeIn="EmployeeAdd,EmployeeDetails"
    enabled.EmployeeAdd="false" .../>
<s:Button id="addBtn"
    includeIn="EmployeeAdd,EmployeeDetails,Employees" .../>
<s:Button id="deleteBtn"
```

```
  includeIn="EmployeeAdd,EmployeeDetails"
  enabled.EmployeeAdd="false" .../>
<s:TextInput id="searchTxt"
  includeIn="EmployeeAdd,EmployeeDetails,Employees" .../>
<s:Button id="searchBtn"
  includeIn="EmployeeAdd,EmployeeDetails,Employees" .../>

<mx:Form includeIn="EmployeeAdd" defaultButton="{button}"
x="63" y="325">
    <mx:FormItem label="Last Name">
        <s:TextInput id="lastnameTextInput"
          text="{employee.lastname}"/>
    </mx:FormItem>
    <mx:FormItem label="First Name">
        <s:TextInput id="firstnameTextInput"
          text="{employee.firstname}"/>
    </mx:FormItem>
    <mx:FormItem label="Title">
        <s:TextInput id="titleTextInput"
          text="{employee.title}"/>
    </mx:FormItem>
    <mx:FormItem label="Department ID">
        <s:TextInput id="departmentidTextInput"
          text="{employee.departmentid}"/>
    </mx:FormItem>
    <mx:FormItem label="Cell Phone">
        <s:TextInput id="cellphoneTextInput"
          text="{employee.cellphone}"/>
    </mx:FormItem>
    <mx:FormItem label="Office Phone">
        <s:TextInput id="officephoneTextInput"
          text="{employee.officephone}"/>
    </mx:FormItem>
    <mx:FormItem label="Email">
        <s:TextInput id="emailTextInput"
          text="{employee.email}"/>
    </mx:FormItem>
</mx:Form>
<mx:Form includeIn="EmployeeAdd" x="372" y="325">
    <mx:FormItem label="Office">
        <s:TextInput id="officeTextInput"
          text="{employee.office}"/>
    </mx:FormItem>
    <mx:FormItem label="Street">
        <s:TextInput id="streetTextInput"
          text="{employee.street}"/>
    </mx:FormItem>
```

```
            <mx:FormItem label="City">
                <s:TextInput id="cityTextInput"
                    text="{employee.city}"/>
            </mx:FormItem>
            <mx:FormItem label="State">
                <s:TextInput id="stateTextInput"
                    text="{employee.state}"/>
            </mx:FormItem>
            <mx:FormItem label="Zipcode">
                <s:TextInput id="zipcodeTextInput"
                    text="{employee.zipcode}"/>
            </mx:FormItem>
            <mx:FormItem label="Photo File">
                <s:TextInput id="photofileTextInput"
                    text="{employee.photofile}"/>
            </mx:FormItem>
            <mx:FormItem>
                <s:Button id="button" label="Add"
                    click="button_clickHandler(event)"/>
            </mx:FormItem>
        </mx:Form>
    </s:Application>
```

Update Data Using a Form

In the previous section, you used an input form to add a new
employee to the database. In this section, you will use the same
form to update the record for an existing employee in the
database.

Step 1: Create a New EmployeeUpdate State

Create the new state based on the EmployeeAdd state. Enable
the Delete button. Change the label of the Add button in the
Form to Update, as shown in Figure 2-7.

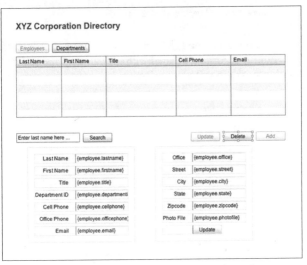

Figure 2-7. Lay out the EmployeeUpdate state as shown here

Step 2: Switch States When the Update Button Is Clicked

Generate a click handler for the main Update button (not the one in the form) that sets the currentState to EmployeeUpdate. Make it the handler for all states.

Your updateBtn Button tag should appear as follows:

```
<s:Button
  includeIn="EmployeeAdd,EmployeeDetails,EmployeeUpdate"
  x="459" y="293" label="Update"
  id="updateBtn" enabled.EmployeeAdd="false"
  enabled.EmployeeUpdate="false"
  click="updateBtn_clickHandler(event)"/>
```

The click event handler should appear as follows:

```
protected function
  updateBtn_clickHandler(event:MouseEvent):void
{
```

```
      currentState="EmployeeUpdate";
  }
```

Run the application and click the Update button. You should
see your input form populated with the values of the selected
employee, as shown in Figure 2-8.

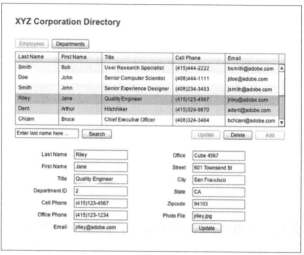

Figure 2-8. View the selected employee details in the input form

Step 3: Submit Changes to the Server

In the EmployeeUpdate state, drag the updateEmployee() operation from the Data/Services panel and drop it on the Update
button in the form. In the handler, pass the employee variable
to updateEmployee() and use conditional logic to call the appropriate service based on whether the employee already has a
nonzero id.

Your handler should appear as follows:

```
protected function
  button_clickHandler(event:MouseEvent):void
{
  employee.lastname = lastnameTextInput.text;
```

```
employee.firstname = firstnameTextInput.text;
employee.title = titleTextInput.text;
employee.departmentid =
  parseInt(departmentidTextInput.text);
employee.cellphone = cellphoneTextInput.text;
employee.officephone = officephoneTextInput.text;
employee.email = emailTextInput.text;
employee.office = officeTextInput.text;
employee.street = streetTextInput.text;
employee.city = cityTextInput.text;
employee.state = stateTextInput.text;
employee.zipcode = zipcodeTextInput.text;
employee.photofile = photofileTextInput.text;
if(employee.id==0){
  createEmployeeResult.token =
    employeeService.createEmployee(employee);
}
else{
  updateEmployeeResult.token =
    employeeService.updateEmployee(employee);
}
}
```

NOTE

This is the handler you have from the previous state with a new service call appended.

Step 4: After the Update, Switch to the EmployeeDetails State

Add a result event attribute to the updateEmployeeResult Call-Responder and generate an event handler. Inside the handler, set currentState to EmployeeDetails.

Your updateEmployeeResult CallResponder should appear as follows:

```
<s:CallResponder id="updateEmployeeResult"
  result="updateEmployeeResult_resultHandler(event)"/>
```

The result event handler should appear as follows:

```
protected function
  updateEmployeeResult_resultHandler(
    event:ResultEvent):void
{
  currentState="EmployeeDetails";
}
```

After the data is updated successfully in the database, the EmployeeDetails state will be shown with the details for this employee.

Run the application and change the properties for an existing employee. Refresh the browser and make sure you see your updated employee data in the DataGrid.

Your code should look like the following (you can download the complete sample code at *www.adobe.com/devnet/flex/test drive/assets/testdrive_modify_data.zip*):

```
<?xml version="1.0" encoding="utf-8"?>
<s:Application ...>
  <fx:Script>
    <![CDATA[
      (...)
      protected function
        button_clickHandler(event:MouseEvent):void
      {
        employee.lastname = lastnameTextInput.text;
        employee.firstname = firstnameTextInput.text;
        (...)
        if(employee.id==0){
          createEmployeeResult.token =
            employeeService.createEmployee(employee);
        }
        else{
          updateEmployeeResult.token =
            employeeService.updateEmployee(employee);
        }
      }
      protected function
        updateBtn_clickHandler(event:MouseEvent):void
      {
        currentState="EmployeeUpdate";
      }
      protected function
```

```
            updateEmployeeResult_resultHandler(
              event:ResultEvent):void
        {
          currentState="EmployeeDetails";
        }
    ]]>
</fx:Script>
<s:states>
    (...)
    <s:State name="EmployeeUpdate"/>
</s:states>
<fx:Declarations>
    (...)
    <s:CallResponder id="updateEmployeeResult"
    result="updateEmployeeResult_resultHandler(event)"/>
</fx:Declarations>
    (...)
<s:Button id="empBtn"
  enabled.EmployeeUpdate="false" .../>
<mx:DataGrid id="empDg"
  includeIn="EmployeeAdd,EmployeeDetails,EmployeeUpdate,
    Employees" .../>

<s:Button id="updateBtn"
  includeIn="EmployeeAdd,EmployeeDetails,EmployeeUpdate"
  enabled.EmployeeUpdate="false"
  click="updateBtn_clickHandler(event)"/>
<s:Button id="addBtn"
  includeIn="EmployeeAdd,EmployeeDetails,EmployeeUpdate,
    Employees"
  enabled.EmployeeAdd="false" .../>
<s:Button id="deleteBtn"
  includeIn="EmployeeAdd,EmployeeDetails,EmployeeUpdate"
  enabled.EmployeeUpdate="true" .../>
<s:TextInput id="searchTxt"
  includeIn="EmployeeAdd,EmployeeDetails,EmployeeUpdate,
    Employees" .../>
<s:Button id="searchBtn"
  includeIn="EmployeeAdd,EmployeeDetails,EmployeeUpdate,
    Employees" .../>
<mx:Form includeIn="EmployeeAdd,EmployeeUpdate" x="63"
  y="325" .../>
<mx:Form includeIn="EmployeeAdd,EmployeeUpdate" x="372"
  y="325" ...>
    (...)
    </mx:FormItem>
        <s:Button id="button" label="Add"
```

```
                    click="button_clickHandler(event)"
                    label.EmployeeUpdate="Update"/>
        </mx:FormItem>
    </mx:Form>
</s:Application>
```

Update Data Using the DataGrid

In the previous section, you used an input form to make changes to an employee record. In this section, you'll let users make changes directly in the DataGrid and propagate those changes to the database.

Step 1: Make the empDg DataGrid Editable in All States

The DataGrid tag should appear as follows:

```
<mx:DataGrid x="36" y="114" id="empDg"
    creationComplete="empDg_creationCompleteHandler(event)"
    dataProvider="{getEmployeesResult.lastResult}"
    width="650"
    includeIn="EmployeeAdd,EmployeeDetails,EmployeeUpdate,
      Employees"
    change="empDg_changeHandler(event)" editable="true">
```

Step 2: Generate an itemEditEnd Event Handler for the DataGrid

Inside the handler, call the updateEmployee() method and pass to it the selected employee, employee.

Your empDg DataGrid tag should appear as follows:

```
<mx:DataGrid x="36" y="114" id="empDg"
    creationComplete="empDg_creationCompleteHandler(event)"
    dataProvider="{getEmployeesResult.lastResult}"
    width="650"
    includeIn="EmployeeAdd,EmployeeDetails,EmployeeUpdate,
      Employees"
    change="empDg_changeHandler(event)"
    editable="true"
    itemEditEnd="empDg_itemEditEndHandler(event)">
```

The `itemEditEnd` event handler should appear as shown here:

```
protected function
  empDg_itemEditEndHandler(event:DataGridEvent):void
{
  employeeService.updateEmployee(employee);
}
```

In this case, you're not going to do anything after the data is successfully updated, so you don't need to specify a CallResponder to handle the results.

Run the application and make changes to the data in the DataGrid (Figure 2-9).

Figure 2-9. Edit employee data in the DataGrid

Refresh the browser page and see that your changes were not saved to the database.

What's going on here is that the `itemEditEnd` event is broadcast after the user has finished editing a cell but before the DataGrid has updated its `dataProvider` with the new value. You need to update the `employee` object with the new property value before sending it to the server.

Step 3: Update employee with the New Value

Inside the handler, set employee[event.dataField] equal to (empDg.itemEditorInstance as mx.controls.TextInput).text.

The itemEditEnd event handler should appear as follows:

```
protected function
  empDg_itemEditEndHandler(event:DataGridEvent):void
{
  employee[event.dataField]=
    (empDg.itemEditorInstance
    as mx.controls.TextInput).text;
  employeeService.updateEmployee(employee);
}
```

event.dataField is a reference to the property of the object being edited, for example title.

NOTE

In ActionScript 3.0, you can access a property one of two ways: using dot syntax (for example, employee.last name); or passing a string between square brackets to the parent (for example, employee[event,dataField]). Dot syntax is typically easier to work with, but in certain cases it can be helpful to access properties by name using strings.

---

empDg.itemEditorInstance is a reference to the component being used in the DataGrid cell to get the new data from the user, in this case a TextInput control that has a text property. The newly entered value will be available in the text property of this object.

Run the application and make changes to the data in the DataGrid. Refresh the browser page and see that your changes are now successfully saved to the database.

In this example, you are sending updates to the server every time the user changes data in one DataGrid cell. If a lot of changes are going to be made, you may want to wait and submit all changes to the server at once.

After you've updated the data, your code should look like the following (you can download the complete sample code at *www.adobe.com/devnet/flex/testdrive/assets/testdrive_mod ify_data.zip*):

```
<?xml version="1.0" encoding="utf-8"?>
<s:Application ...>
  <fx:Script>
    <![CDATA[
      (...)
      import mx.events.DataGridEvent;

      protected function
        empDg_itemEditEndHandler(event:DataGridEvent):void
      {
        employee[event.dataField]=(empDg.itemEditorInstance
          as mx.controls.TextInput).text;
          employeeService.updateEmployee(employee);
      }
    ]]>
  </fx:Script>
  (...)
  <mx:DataGrid x="36" y="114" id="empDg"
    creationComplete="empDg_creationCompleteHandler(event)"
    dataProvider="{getEmployeesResult.lastResult}"
    width="650" includeIn="EmployeeAdd,EmployeeDetails,
    EmployeeUpdate,Employees"
    change="empDg_changeHandler(event)" editable="true"
    itemEditEnd="empDg_itemEditEndHandler(event)">
    <mx:columns>
      <mx:DataGridColumn headerText="Last Name"
        dataField="lastname"/>
      <mx:DataGridColumn headerText="First Name"
        dataField="firstname"/>
      <mx:DataGridColumn headerText="Title"
        dataField="title" width="170"/>
      <mx:DataGridColumn headerText="Cell Phone"
        dataField="cellphone"/>
      <mx:DataGridColumn headerText="Email"
        dataField="email" width="130"/>
    </mx:columns>
```

```
    </mx:DataGrid>
    (...)
</s:Application>
```

Delete Data

In this section, you will delete data from the database.

Step 1: Call the Service deleteEmployee() Operation

In EmployeeDetails view, drag the deleteEmployee() operation
out and drop it on the Delete button. In the newly generated
handler, pass the id of the selected employee.

Your handler should appear as follows:

```
protected function
  deleteBtn_clickHandler(event:MouseEvent):void
{
  deleteEmployeeResult.token =
    employeeService.deleteEmployee(employee.id);
}
```

Your deleteBtn Button tag should appear as follows:

```
<s:Button
  includeIn="EmployeeAdd,EmployeeDetails,EmployeeUpdate"
  x="537" y="293" label="Delete "
  id="deleteBtn" enabled.EmployeeAdd="false"
  enabled.EmployeeUpdate="true"
  click="deleteBtn_clickHandler(event)"/>
```

Step 2: Update the Local Data

Add a result event attribute to the deleteEmployeeResult Call-
Responder and generate an event handler. Inside the handler,
set currentState to Employees and use the removeItemAt()
method to remove the employee from the DataGrid
dataProvider.

Your `deleteEmployeeResult` CallResponder should appear as follows:

```
<s:CallResponder id="deleteEmployeeResult"
  result="deleteEmployeeResult_resultHandler(event)"/>
```

The `result` event handler should appear as follows:

```
protected function
  deleteEmployeeResult_resultHandler(
    event:ResultEvent):void
{
  empDg.dataProvider.removeItemAt(empDg.selectedIndex);
  currentState="Employees";
}
```

When you call the `deleteEmployee()` service operation, the employee is deleted from the database, but not from the collection of data being displayed in the DataGrid. You need to remove it from the data displayed in the DataGrid by removing it from the DataGrid's `dataProvider`.

`removeItemAt()` is a method of the Flex `ArrayCollection` class. When the employee data was initially retrieved from the server, Flex stored the data as an ArrayCollection of Employee objects as the DataGrid `dataProvider`.

Run the application and delete an employee—preferably one of the new ones you added. Refresh the browser and make sure you no longer see the employee you deleted in the DataGrid.

Congratulations! You have performed all your data CRUD from a Flex application: you created, read, updated, and deleted data from the database.

When you complete this module, your code should look like the following (you can download the complete sample code at *www.adobe.com/devnet/flex/testdrive/assets/testdrive_mod ify_data.zip*):

```
<?xml version="1.0" encoding="utf-8"?>
<s:Application ...>
  <fx:Script>
    <![CDATA[
      (...)
      protected function
```

```
              deleteBtn_clickHandler(event:MouseEvent):void
            {
              deleteEmployeeResult.token =
                employeeService.deleteEmployee(employee.id);
            }
            protected function
              deleteEmployeeResult_resultHandler(
                event:ResultEvent):void
            {
              empDg.dataProvider.removeItemAt(
                empDg.selectedIndex);
              currentState="Employees";
            }
        ]]>
    </fx:Script>
    <fx:Declarations>
        (...)
        <s:CallResponder id="deleteEmployeeResult"
        result="deleteEmployeeResult_resultHandler(event)"/>
    </fx:Declarations>
    (...)
    <s:Button id="deleteBtn"
      includeIn="EmployeeAdd,EmployeeDetails,EmployeeUpdate"
      x="537" y="293" label="Delete "
      enabled.EmployeeAdd="false"
      enabled.EmployeeUpdate="true"
      click="deleteBtn_clickHandler(event)"/>
    (...)
</s:Application>
```

CHAPTER 3

Test and Debug Your Code

In the previous two chapters, you built Flex applications that retrieve, display, and modify data from a database. In this chapter, you will test and debug your code. No code is written in this chapter—the exercises here execute the code in the file *TestDrive_test_debug_2.mxml*, which is included in the sample code download at *www.adobe.com/devnet/flex/testdrive/assets/ testdrive_test_debug.zip*.

Test Server-Side Code

In this section, you will use the Flash Builder Test Operation to test your server-side code—even before writing any Flex code. This is useful to make sure your server-side operations are all working before you call them in your application.

Step 1: Test a Service Operation That Returns Data

Right-click the getEmployees() operation in the Data/Services view and select Test Operation. Click the Test button in the Test Operation view.

You will see all the return data displayed in the Test Operation view (Figure 3-1).

NOTE

The Test Operation window may open in the bottom pane of your Flash Builder 4 workspace. To expand it, either drag the boundary higher to expand the size of the bottom pane or double-click the Test Operation tab to maximize it.

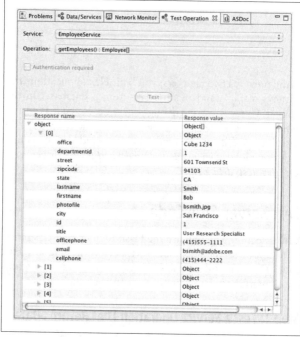

Figure 3-1. The Test Operation tab displays the return data

Step 2: Test a Service Operation That Requires an Input Parameter

Select the `getEmployeesById()` operation from the drop-down list in the Test Operation tab. Enter a value for the argument and click Test. The `getEmployeesById()` operation is invoked with the value you specified, and the return data is displayed in the Test Operation tab (Figure 3-2).

Step 3: Test a Service Operation That Requires a Complex Input Parameter

Select the `createEmployee()` operation in the Test Operation tab. Click in the Enter Value field and click the ellipsis button. A pop-up window similar to the one shown in Figure 3-3 will appear for you to enter input data. You can pass an object literal to the server using this pop-up window. However, because you know the value object's type in this case, you can close this window without entering anything and configure the object elsewhere. Close this window.

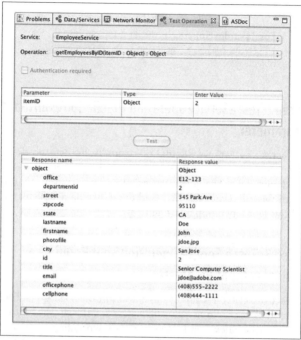

Figure 3-2. Test the getEmployeesById() service operation

NOTE

For Java developers: Your Input Argument window will look different because your method already knows it needs an Employee object. You can skip Steps 4 and 5 below and just enter test values here (as shown in Figure 3-5) and then test the operation. Be sure to enter integers for id and departmentid and only two characters for state. It doesn't matter what id you specify, it will not be used; the database will automatically generate a value for it when the data is inserted.

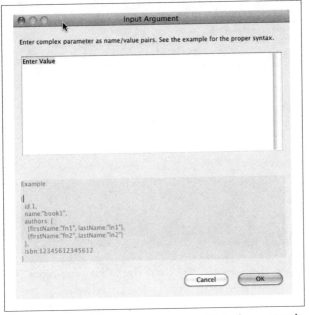

Figure 3-3. You will be asked for an input object when testing the createEmployee() operation

Step 4: Configure the createEmployee() Operation Return Type

Return to the Data/Services view, right-click `createEm ployee()`, and select Configure Return Type. In the dialog box, autodetect from sample data, change the type from Object to Employee, and click in the Enter Value field (Figure 3-4). Click the ellipsis button that appears and enter values for each Employee field (Figure 3-5). Be sure to enter integers for `departmentid` and `id`, and only two characters for `state`. It does not matter what `id` you specify because it will not be used; the database will automatically generate a value for it when the data is inserted.

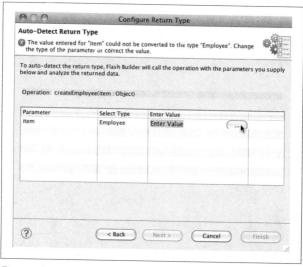

Figure 3-4. Specify the data type when configuring the createEmployee() return type

You should now see parameter and return types (`Employee` and `int`, respectively) specified for the `createEmployee()` operation in the Data/Services panel.

Step 5: Test the createEmployee() Operation Again

Right-click `createEmployee()` in the Data/Services view and select Test Operation. Click the Test button in the Test Operation view. This time, you will see the test values you specified while configuring the return type already entered in the Enter Value field.

After you test the operation, you should see an integer displayed as the response value, as shown in Figure 3-6. A new employee was successfully added to the database. If you run your application again, you will see this new employee in the DataGrid.

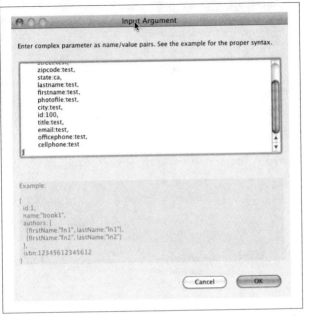

Figure 3-5. Specify input arguments when configuring the createEmployee() return type

Trace Network Traffic

In this section, you will use the Flash Builder Network Monitor to monitor the traffic between your application and the server. This lets you quickly and easily see the data being sent to and returned from the server.

Step 1: Enable the Network Monitor

Open the Network Monitor view, enable the Network Monitor (Figure 3-7), and run your application.

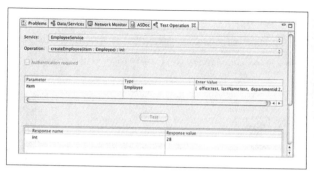

Figure 3-6. Test the createEmployee() service operation

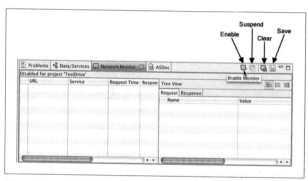

Figure 3-7. Enable the Network Monitor

Before you do anything in the application, return to Flash Builder and look at the Network Monitor. You will see two requests: client_ping and getEmployees (see Figure 3-8). The Flex data service uses the client_ping operation to check the server's responsiveness before it sends any actual requests. The getEmployees operation is the initial call to the server-side getEmployees() method to populate the DataGrid. The time each request took is also displayed.

Figure 3-8. View the network traffic between the application and the server

Step 2: View the getEmployees() Response

Select the getEmployees operation in the Network Monitor's lefthand panel and look at the request and response data for it in the righthand panel (Figure 3-9). The return type is Action Message Format (AMF), a binary format Flash Remoting uses to make calls to server-side classes.

NOTE

For Java developers: Each of your objects will be of type `services.Employee`.

Notice the three buttons in the upper-right corner to view the data in tree, raw, or hex formats.

Step 3: View Network Traffic Data for Additional Operations

Return to your application in the browser and add, update, and delete data. Return to the Network Monitor and explore the data for the service calls. When you are done, disable the Network Monitor. Be sure to look at the request data sent to the server when an employee is created or updated (Figure 3-10).

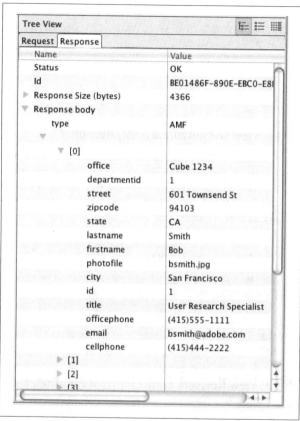

Figure 3-9. View data returned from the getEmployees() operation

---

NOTE

For Java developers: Your object will be of type
`services.Employee`.

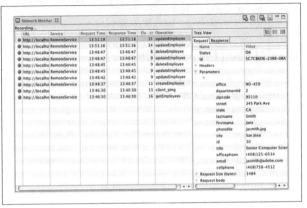

Figure 3-10. View request data for an updateEmployee() operation call

Trace Variables

In this section, you will use the Flash Builder debugger and the
trace() function to display values of variables at runtime. To
debug applications, you must have the debug version of Flash
Player installed for your browser. Debug versions of Flash
Player are installed when Flash Builder is installed.

Step 1: Trace Employee-Related Variables

Inside the DataGrid itemEditEnd handler, called empDg_itemE
ditEndHandler(), use the trace() function to display
employee.id, employee, and empDg.dataProvider.

Your handler should appear as follows:

```
protected function
  empDg_itemEditEndHandler(event:DataGridEvent):void
{
  trace(employee.id);
  trace(employee);
  trace(empDg.dataProvider);
```

```
employee[event.dataField]=(empDg.itemEditorInstance
  as mx.controls.TextInput).text;
employeeService.updateEmployee(employee);
```

Step 2: Debug the Application

Click the Debug button or select Run→Debug TestDrive to debug the application. Edit a cell, then return to Flash Builder
and access the Console view.

For the first trace of **employee.id**, you will see the value for the
employee you edited (as shown in Figure 3-11). For the second
trace of **employee**, you will see [object Employee], indicating it
is a complex object of type Employee; however, you won't see
any of the property values. For the third trace of **empDg.data
Provider**, you will see a comma-delimited list of Employee objects, indicating it is an array of Employee objects, but again,
you will not see individual property values.

*Figure 3-11. View employee-related variables traced in the Console
view*

Step 3: Stop the Debugger and Switch Perspectives

Click one of the red Terminate buttons, then click the Flash
and Flash Debug buttons in the upper-right corner (Figure 3-12) to switch between the development and debugging
perspectives. You should have the development perspective
open for this exercise. If you do not see both buttons, click the
left edge of the tab and drag it to the left until you see them.

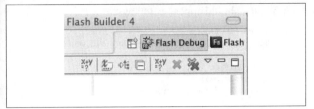

Figure 3-12. Switch between the development and debugging perspectives

Step 4: Trace Event-Related Variables

Inside the DataGrid `itemEditEnd` handler, trace `event` and `event.dataField`. Debug the application and edit a cell.

For the first trace of `event`, you will see [Event type="itemEnd" bubbles=false cancelable=true eventPhase=2]. This indicates it is an object of type Event, and some of its properties and their values are listed (as shown in Figure 3-13). For the second trace of `event.dataField`, you will see the name of the Employee property you just edited in the DataGrid. When you are finished, stop the debugger.

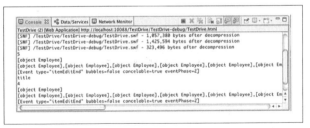

Figure 3-13. View event-related variables traced in the Console view

Step 5: Trace the Value of the Edited DataGrid Cell

Trace `employee[event.dataField]` before and after the assignment statement. Debug the application and edit a cell.

Your handler should appear as follows:

```
protected function
  empDg_itemEditEndHandler(event:DataGridEvent):void
{
  trace(employee.id);
  trace(employee);
  trace(empDg.dataProvider);

  trace(event);
  trace(event.dataField);
  trace(employee[event.dataField]);
  employee[event.dataField]=
    (empDg.itemEditorInstance
     as mx.controls.TextInput).text;
  trace(employee[event.dataField]);
  employeeService.updateEmployee(employee);
}
```

You should see both the initial and final values of the property you edited in the DataGrid (Figure 3-14). When the itemEditEnd event is broadcast, the DataGrid dataProvider has not yet been updated with the new data.

Figure 3-14. View the value of the edited cell traced in the Console view

When you are finished, stop the debugger. Your code should look like the following:

```
<?xml version="1.0" encoding="utf-8"?>
<s:Application ...>
  <fx:Script>
    <![CDATA[
      (...)
      protected function
        empDg_itemEditEndHandler(event:DataGridEvent):void
```

```
      {
        trace(employee.id);
        trace(employee);
        trace(empDg.dataProvider);
        trace(event);
        trace(event.dataField);
        trace(employee[event.dataField]);
          employee[event.dataField]=
          (empDg.itemEditorInstance
          as mx.controls.TextInput).text;
        trace(employee[event.dataField]);
          employeeService.updateEmployee(employee);
      }
    ]]>
  </fx:Script>
   (...)
</s:Application>
```

Use Breakpoints

Tracing is a useful tool, but for even a medium-sized application it may not be feasible to trace out everything you want to monitor. Your Console window can become cluttered with lines of text, making it difficult to find the line you're looking for as you debug. It is often a better practice to use breakpoints to examine your application during runtime.

In this section, you will use the Flash Builder debugger to debug your Flex code. You will add breakpoints to stop code execution inside an event handler and look at the values of variables as you step through your code.

Step 1: Add a Breakpoint

Locate the marker bar to the left of the line numbers. If the line numbers feature is not visible, turn line numbers on in Eclipse. Double-click the marker bar next to the first line of code inside the DataGrid `itemEditEnd` handler, `empDg_itemEditEndHandler` (shown in Figure 3-15). Debug the application and edit a cell.

```
   97⊖            protected function empDg_itemEditEndHandler(event:DataGridEvent):void
   98            {
 ● 99                trace(employee.id);
  100                trace(employee);
  101                trace(empDg.dataProvider);
  102                trace(event):
```

Figure 3-15. Select the first line of code in the empDg_itemEditEndHandler

After you edit a cell in the browser, the Flash Builder will be displayed automatically (or you may see it flashing in your dock or taskbar and need to navigate to it manually), and you will see an arrow next to the first line of code inside the handler, indicating that code execution has stopped there (Figure 3-16).

```
   97⊖            protected function empDg_itemEditEndHandler(event:DataGridEvent):void
   98            {
 ⬢ 99                trace(employee.id);
  100                trace(employee);
  101                trace(empDg.dataProvider);
  102                trace(event);
```

Figure 3-16. Locate where code execution stopped

Step 2: Look at Variables in the Variables View

Variables view will display two variables, this and event (Figure 3-17). this is a reference to the application itself, and event is the variable passed to empDg_itemEditEndHandler(). Locate the event.dataField property, the reference to the field you edited in the DataGrid.

Step 3: Look at the Inherited Properties of the event Object

Drill down into the event object's inherited properties and then into the currentTarget property (Figure 3-18).

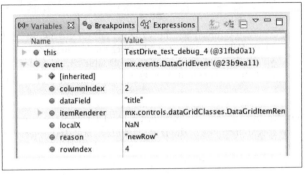

Figure 3-17. View variables in the Variables view

`currentTarget` is a reference to the `empDg` DataGrid, the object listening for the event that was broadcast. Drill down into the `currentTarget` object's properties and locate the `dataProvider` property. The `dataProvider` is an ArrayCollection (a Flex-managed array) of Employee objects. Look at the values for one of the Employee objects.

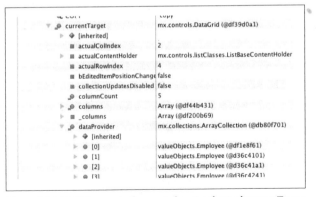

Figure 3-18. Drill down into the event object's inherited currentTarget property

Locate the `currentTarget` object's `itemEditorInstance` property. It is an instance of the `TextInput` class, and that object has
a `text` property. In your code, you updated the `employee` object's property with the value contained in this value:
`(empDg.itemEditorInstance as mx.controls.TextInput).text`.

Step 4: Step into Your Code

Click the Step Into button (Figure 3-19) 10 or more times and
watch as the debugger steps through your code. Stop when in
the debugger gets to a different file and click the Step Return
button to return code execution back to your MXML file. Various files will open and close as code in other classes executes.

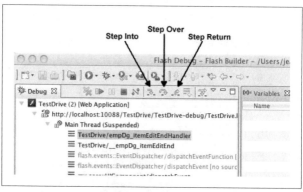

*Figure 3-19. Use the buttons in the Debug view toolbar to step through
code*

You can continue to step through code and watch the values of variables in the Variables view, but if you are interested in watching the value of one or more particular variables, you can explicitly watch them instead.

Step 5: Watch the employee[event.dataField] Variable

Select `employee[event.dataField]` anywhere inside the `empDg_itemEditEndHandler()` handler and select Create Watch Expression. You should see the expression listed in the Expressions view, as shown in Figure 3-20.

Figure 3-20. Create a watch expression

Step 6: Step Through Code and Watch the Expression Change Value

Use the Step Into, Step Over, and Step Return buttons and see the value of the watched expression change from the initial value of the DataGrid cell to the edited value (Figure 3-21).

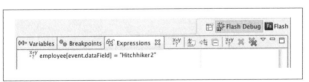

Figure 3-21. Watch an expression change value; in this case, "Hitchhiker" changes to "Hitchhiker2"

Stop the debugger.

Congratulations! You've learned to use the Flash Builder Test
Operation to test your server-side code, the Flash Builder
Network Monitor to trace network traffic between your Flex
application and the server, and the Flash Builder debugger to
debug your Flex application.

When you complete this exercise, your code should look like
the following (you can download the complete sample code at
*www.adobe.com/devnet/flex/testdrive/assets/testdrive_test_de
bug.zip*):

```
<?xml version="1.0" encoding="utf-8"?>
<s:Application ...>
   <fx:Script>
      <![CDATA[
         (...)
         protected function
           empDg_itemEditEndHandler(
             event:DataGridEvent):void
         {
           trace(employee.id);
           trace(employee);
           trace(empDg.dataProvider);
           trace(event);
           trace(event.dataField);
           trace(employee[event.dataField]);
             employee[event.dataField]=
             (empDg.itemEditorInstance
             as mx.controls.TextInput).text;
           trace(employee[event.dataField]);
             employeeService.updateEmployee(employee);
         }
      ]]>
   </fx:Script>
   (...)
</s:Application>
```

CHAPTER 4

Deploy Your Application to a Web Server

In the previous three chapters, you learned to build and debug a Flex application. In this chapter, you will learn to deploy your application to a web server.

Create a Release Version

The first task is to create a release version of the application. When you are developing your application, a debug version of your application is created and stored in the project's *bin-debug* folder. This SWF file includes additional code and metadata that the debugger uses. When you are done debugging and ready to deploy, you need to create a release build of the application—a smaller, nondebug version of the SWF file.

Step 1: Create a Release Build

In Flash Builder, Select Project→Export Release Build. In the Export Release Build wizard, select your project and application and specify where you want the release build saved. Figure 4-1 shows an example for a local PHP Zend server.

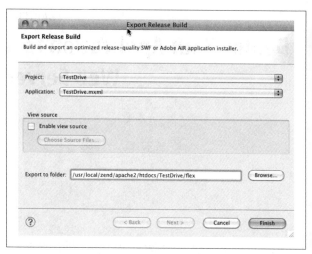

Figure 4-1. Creating a release build for a local PHP Zend server

If you look in the Package Explorer, you will now see a *bin-release* folder in your project, like the one shown in Figure 4-2. This is a pointer to the export folder you just specified.

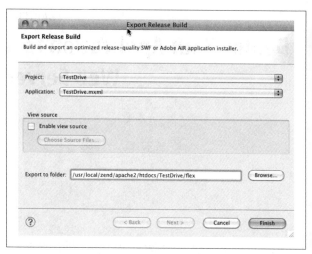

Figure 4-2. View the bin-release folder

The *bin-debug* and *bin-release* folders contain many files in addition to the SWF file. You will learn about these different files later in the chapter.

Step 2: Compare Application File Sizes

Right-click the SWF file in the *bin-debug* directory and select Properties to view its location and size. Repeat for the SWF file in the *bin-release* folder.

The release SWF file is typically 100 KB or less in size.

Include Your Application on a Web Page

In this section, you will learn how to include your Flex application on a web page and deploy it to a web server. You will learn what code you need to add to a web page to load your Flex application and what additional files you need to place on the web server along with the SWF file.

To view your application, the user needs Flash Player—more specifically, a particular version of Flash Player. This means the web page that embeds your application must also contain code to check for the presence of the minimum required version of Flash Player and code to help users upgrade or get Flash Player if their system does not meet the requirements.

Step 1: Look at the html-template Files

Look at the files used to generate your browser-embedded application (shown in Figure 4-3).

The files you see in this folder will depend upon your project settings.

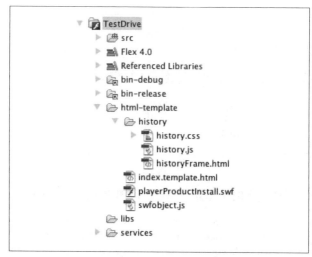

Figure 4-3. View the html-template files

By default, when you build your application, these template files are used to generate the HTML file and other files that are placed in the *bin-debug* and *bin-release* folders. They contain variables that are populated by project properties or application tag attributes. The next two steps discuss the purpose of each file.

Step 2: Open TestDrive.html

The *TestDrive.html* file is in the *bin-release* folder. Look at the generated code for embedding the Flex application.

The primary code for checking for the presence and minimum version of Flash Player is provided by SWFObject 2, a standards-based library for embedding SWF files in HTML pages. The following code includes the library in the web page:

```
<script type="text/javascript"
  src="swfobject.js"></script>
```

The SWF file is embedded by calling the `embed()` method of `swfobject`, as follows:

```
swfobject.embedSWF(
  "TestDrive.swf", "flashContent", "100%", "100%",
  swfVersionStr, xiSwfUrlStr, flashvars, params,
  attributes);
```

The first argument is the location of the SWF file.

The second argument is the name of alternate content (the `id` of a `div` tag defined further down in the code) to display if Flash Player is not available.

The third and fourth arguments specify the height and width of the application. By default, these are set to 100% in the generated HTML wrapper so the application takes up the entire browser window. To change the application's size—for example, to take up a certain amount of space in an existing HTML page—change these arguments to other absolute or relative values.

The fifth argument specifies the minimum required version of Flash Player. Flex 4 applications require Flash Player 10.0.0 or later.

The sixth argument adds Express Installation, a quick, seamless way for users to upgrade their version of Flash Player if it does not meet the minimum requirements. This argument is set equal to an empty string (for no Express Installation) or to the location of the SWF file providing this functionality: *playerProductInstall.swf*. Both of these values are set in JavaScript code before the `embed()` call.

The last three arguments pass data to the application and set properties for the application. Use the `flashvars` object to pass data to the Flex application from the containing web page. Use the `params` and `attributes` objects to specify how the SWF file should appear in the browser, including its quality, alignment, scale, transparency, and more.

Finally, take a look at the `noscript` tag, which is executed in browsers with JavaScript disabled. It contains two `object` tags that provide a nonJavaScript way to embed a SWF file:

```
<noscript>
  <object
    classid="clsid:D27CDB6E-AE6D-11cf-96B8-444553540000"
    width="100%" height="100%" id="TestDrive">
    <param name="movie" value="TestDrive.swf" />
    <param name="quality" value="high" />
    <param name="bgcolor" value="#ffffff" />
    <param name="allowScriptAccess" value="sameDomain" />
    <param name="allowFullScreen" value="true" />
    <!--[if !IE]>-->
      <object type="application/x-shockwave-flash"
        data="TestDrive.swf" width="100%" height="100%">
        <param name="quality" value="high" />
        <param name="bgcolor" value="#ffffff" />
        <param name="allowScriptAccess"
          value="sameDomain" />
        <param name="allowFullScreen" value="true" />
    <!--<![endif]-->
    <!--[if gte IE 6]>-->
      <p> Either scripts and active content are not
          permitted to run or Adobe Flash Player
          version 10.0.0 or greater is not installed.
      </p>
    <!--<![endif]-->
    <a href="/go/getflashplayer"><img
      src="/images/shared/download_buttons/
        get_flash_player.gif"
      alt="Get Adobe Flash Player" /></a>
    <!--[if !IE]>-->
    </object>
    <!--<![endif]-->
  </object>
</noscript>
```

The `object` tag with the `classid` is for use with Internet Explorer and browsers that implement Flash Player as a Flash ActiveX control. The second `object` tag is for use with browsers that implement Flash Player as a plug-in, such as Firefox, Safari, or Chrome. Use `param` tags to set SWF parameters for both.

If you want to change SWF properties, make sure you set identical parameter values for the `swfobject` and both of the `noscript object` tags.

If you want to embed your application in an existing web page and not use the default wrapper, make sure all of this code (or equivalent functionality) exists in that web page.

Step 3: Look at the bin-release Files

When you deploy your application to a web server, to be on the safe side, you can just move all the files located in the *bin-release* folder (Figure 4-4) to the production server. Take a look at each of these files now, though, so you can determine if you actually need them all.

Every Flex application uses at least part of the Flex framework. To minimize your SWF file size and download times, the framework code is not compiled into your application. Instead, it is provided separately as a group of Adobe authenticated Runtime Shared Libraries (RSLs), which you only have to download once. Flash Player caches the RSLs and you can use them with any Flex application. These are all the SWZ files you see in the project *bin* folders.

When a user requests an application that uses Adobe RSLs (which all Flex 4 applications do by default), if Flash Player already has the appropriate version of the framework files cached locally, it uses them. Otherwise, Flash Player downloads them from the Adobe website and caches them locally. This means you do not have to deploy these SWZ files to your web server. You can, though, if you want them on your server for failover or if you're deploying an application to an Internet-restricted environment.

Table 4-1 lists and describes each of the files in the *bin* folders.

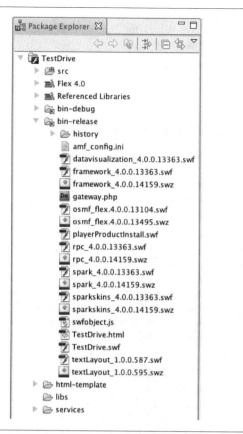

Figure 4-4. View the files in the bin-release folder

Table 4-1. Files contained in the bin folders

File	Description	Deploy?
history folder	Includes JavaScript, CSS, and HTML pages that are used for deep-linking, which lets users navigate the application	Yes, if your application uses deep-linking.

File	Description	Deploy?
	interactions with the browser's Forward and Back buttons and enables the creation of custom URLs for bookmarking.	
datavisualization_x.swz	RSL for the data visualization components, including charts and advanced grids.	No, provided on Adobe servers.
framework_x.swz	RSL for core Flex framework and MX components.	No, provided on Adobe servers.
osmf_flex_x.swz	RSL for the open source media framework used primarily with the Spark Video Player component.	No, provided on Adobe servers.
PlayerProductInstall.swf	The SWF file used with swfobject for Express Installation—a quick, seamless way for users to upgrade Flash Player.	Always, unless you disable Express Installation.
rpc_x.swz	RSL for data services that make HTTP, web service, or Flash Remoting calls.	No, provided on Adobe servers.
spark_x.swz	RSL for Spark components.	No, provided on Adobe servers.
sparkskins_x.swz	RSL for skins for MX components.	No, provided on Adobe servers.
swfobject.js	SWFObject 2 code for detecting Flash Player and embedding a SWF file in a web page.	Always, unless you do not use swfobject to embed your SWF file in a web page.
TestDrive.html	The HTML page that embeds the Flex application.	Deploy this file or another web server page that embeds the SWF file and checks for the minimum required version of Flash Player.
TestDrive.swf	Your application!	Always.

File	Description	Deploy?
textLayout_x.swz	RSL for the Text Layout Framework used by the Spark text controls.	No, provided on Adobe servers.

NOTE

For PHP developers: You will also see an *amf_config.ini* file and a *gateway.php* file in the bin folders. These files are used when your application makes service calls (discussed later in the chapter).

Step 4: Change the Project Settings So History Files Are Not Generated

To prevent history files from being generated in your project, take the following steps:

1. Select Project→Properties, go to Flex Compiler, uncheck "Enable integration with browser navigation," and click Apply.

2. Click OK in the pop-up window that appears to warn you that files in the *html-template* directory will be deleted or overwritten.

NOTE

If you've customized *index.template.html* to do something like pass in **flashvars** to the application, you will need to reenter that information in the template file.

---

3. Select Project→Clean.

4. Take a look at the *bin-debug* folder again. You should no longer see the history folder.

When you clean a project, all of the files in the *bin-debug* folder are deleted and then built again from scratch.

Deploy Service Code

In this section, you will take a look at where you need to place your service code—that is, your server-side class files—so your Flex application can access them. Because this location depends on the application server you're using, refer to the following sections for your server-side technology—PHP, ColdFusion, or Java.

PHP

When moving a Flex and PHP application to a production server, you must do the following:

- Ensure the Zend Framework is installed on the server.
- Ensure the *gateway.php* and *amf-config.ini* files are in the same folder as the SWF file.
- Ensure the PHP classes the Flex application calls are located in one of the directories specified in the *amf-config.ini* file.
- Update the *amf-config.ini* file to reflect the locations of the production server's web root and Zend Framework.

Step 1: In Flash Builder, browse the generated EmployeeService file

This is the *services.employeeservice._Super_EmployeeService.as* file. Locate the source, endpoint, and destination assignment statements (Figure 4-5).

When you create a data service in Flash Builder, you specify the location of the PHP class to call. The name of this class is hardcoded in this generated service file, but its location is not.

```
 66            _serviceControl.convertResultHandler = com.adobe.:
 67            _serviceControl.source = "EmployeeService";
 68            _serviceControl.endpoint = "gateway.php";
 69            _serviceControl.destination = "EmployeeService";
 70
```

Figure 4-5. Locate the code specifying the location of the PHP class

Notice that the endpoint, the file to invoke, is set equal to the
gateway.php file located in the same directory as the SWF file.
Flash Builder will create this file if it does not already exist.
When you deploy your files to a web server, ensure the *gate-
way.php* file remains in the same folder as the SWF file.

If the PHP class ever changes, you can refresh the data service
in the Data/Services view to update the generated files. If you
rename the PHP class, though, you will need to re-create the
data service.

Step 2: Open the generated Flash Remoting files

In the *bin-debug* (or *bin-release*) folder, open *gateway.php* and
amf-config.ini.

gateway.php is the endpoint for all Flash Remoting requests
from your application. It (along with the Zend Framework)
handles the service request, invoking the correct class method
and handling all data translation and packaging. It references
a configuration file, *amf_config.ini*, which sets the location of
the web root, the location of the Zend Framework, a production flag (to suppress debug messages), and the directories to
look in for classes specified in service calls:

```
[zend]
;set the absolute location path of webroot directory,
  example:
;Windows: C:\apache\www
;MAC/UNIX: /user/apache/www
webroot =/usr/local/zend/apache2/htdocs/

;set the absolute location path of zend installation
  directory,
example:
```

```
;Windows: C:\apache\PHPFrameworks\ZendFramework\library
;MAC/UNIX:
  /user/apache/PHPFrameworks/ZendFramework/library
;zend_path =

[zendamf]
amf.production = true
amf.directories[]=TestDrive/services
```

Because the directories that contain classes used in Flash Remoting service calls are listed here, when you deploy your Flex application to a web server, any PHP classes it calls must still be located in one of the directories specified here. Otherwise, you need to update this file so it lists the new service file location. You should also set amf.production to true to suppress debug messages.

Of course, you also need to update the *amf_config.ini* file to reflect the locations of the web root and the Zend Framework on the production server.

Step 3: Open the PHP web root folder

Locate the *ZendFramework* folder. Ensure the Zend Framework is installed on your production server and that the correct location for it is specified in the *amf-config.ini* file.

ColdFusion

You can place your Flex application and the ColdFusion components (CFCs) it calls anywhere in */ColdFusion/wwwroot/*. They don't have to be in the same folder and they can be in any subfolders. The relative path between them does not matter. The CFCs, however, do need to be located in the same location as they were on the development server relative to the web root.

If you want to put the CFCs outside the web root, create a ColdFusion mapping pointing to that location and specify the use of ColdFusion mappings in the configuration file used for Flash Remoting requests.

Step 1: Locate the Flash Remoting configuration file

Select Project→Properties and select Flex Compiler. You will
see the following compiler argument:

```
-services "/Applications/ColdFusion9/wwwroot/WEB-INF/flex
          /services-config.xml"
```

This compiler argument was added when you created the
project (as a ColdFusion project using Flash Remoting). It
specifies the location of the *services-config.xml* file that contains the details for how the communication between the application and the server should occur and which server-side
classes handle the requests and translation and packaging of
data.

Step 2: Open the services-config.xml file

This file is located in */ColdFusion9/wwwroot/WEB-INF/flex/*.
Locate the `coldfusion` tag in the `my-cfamf` channel definition.

You will see settings specifying whether ColdFusion uses mappings to find CFCs, whether public as well as remote methods
will be accessible, and how to handle the case of property values when converting between ColdFusion and ActionScript
(since ColdFusion is case-insensitive and ActionScript is
case-sensitive):

```
<coldfusion>
    <access>
        <use-mappings>true</use-mappings>
        <method-access-level>remote</method-access-level>
    </access>
    <use-accessors>true</use-accessors>
    <use-structs>false</use-structs>
    <property-case>
        <force-cfc-lowercase>true
        </force-cfc-lowercase>
        <force-query-lowercase>true
        </force-query-lowercase>
        <force-struct-lowercase>true
        </force-struct-lowercase>
    </property-case>
</coldfusion>
```

Near the top of the file, you will also see the following include statement for a *remoting-config.xml* file:

```
<service-include file-path="remoting-config.xml" />
```

NOTE

If you are not using ColdFusion 9, your configuration files will look slightly different. Refer to your ColdFusion documentation for details.

Step 3: Open the remoting-config.xml file

This file is located in */ColdFusion9/wwwroot/WEB-INF/flex/*. Locate the ColdFusion destination.

This is the default destination Flex applications use for calls to any ColdFusion component; the wildcard (*) character for the source means Flex can call a CFC in any location. In this case, you must specify the location of the CFC in the Flex application file:

```
<destination id="ColdFusion">
    <channels>
        <channel ref="my-cfamf"/>
    </channels>
    <properties>
        <source>*</source>
    </properties>
</destination>
```

NOTE

You can also specify named destinations that are associated with a particular CFC endpoint.

Step 4: In Flash Builder, browse the generated EmployeeService file

This is the *services.employeeservice._Super_EmployeeService.as* file. Locate the source and destination assignment statements (Figure 4-6).

When you create a data service in Flash Builder, you specify the location of the CFC to call, and this value is hardcoded in this generated service file. Notice that the destination is set to ColdFusion, the name of the default destination in the remoting-config file, and the source is the path to the CFC from the web root.

If the CFC ever changes, you can refresh the data service from the Data/Services view to update the generated files. If you move or rename the CFC, though, you will need to re-create the data service. This means that when you deploy your Flex application to a web server, any CFCs it calls must be located in the same location as they were on the development server relative to the web root.

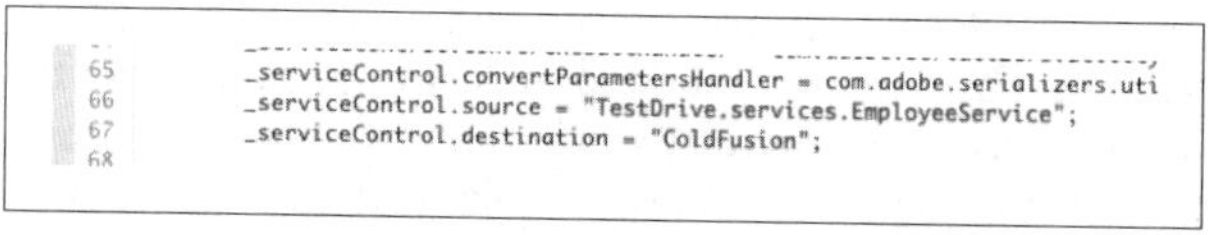

```
65      _serviceControl.convertParametersHandler = com.adobe.serializers.uti
66      _serviceControl.source = "TestDrive.services.EmployeeService";
67      _serviceControl.destination = "ColdFusion";
68
```

Figure 4-6. Locate the code specifying the location of the CFC

Java

When moving a Flex and Java application to a production server, you must set up BlazeDS for the web application you are adding your Flex application to. You must also edit the remoting-config.xml file so it has a destination with the name you used in your application and points to the correct Java class.

Step 1: Locate the required BlazeDS files

Open the /testdrive/ folder.

If you are creating a new web application, you can just package and deploy your development application. Otherwise, you need to set up BlazeDS for the production web application. You can get the necessary files from the development web application or by downloading the BlazeDS WAR file from

http://opensource.adobe.com/wiki/display/blazeds/Downloads
and getting them from the extracted WAR file.

Open the */testdrive/WEB-INF/lib* folder. Copy all the JAR files
to the *lib* folder of the production web application (Figure 4-7). Most of these files handle communication between
Flash Player and the server, except *flex-rds-server.jar* and
derby.jar. The *flex-rds-server.jar* file is new to BlazeDS 4
(which, at the time of writing, is in beta) and Flash Builder uses
it at development time to create a data service by introspecting
the server-side classes. The *derby.jar* file is, of course, for the
Apache Derby embedded database that this application uses.

Open the */testdrive/WEB-INF/flex* folder. Copy this folder to
the *WEB-INF* folder of the production web application. It contains all the BlazeDS configuration files.

Open the */testdrive/WEB-INF/web.xml* file. Copy this file to the
production *WEB-INF* folder as well. If the production web application already has a *web.xml* file configured, you can just
copy the servlet mapping for `MessageBrokerServlet` and listener
for `HttpFlexSession` using the following code:

```
<!-- Http Flex Session attribute and binding listener
support -->
  <listener>
      <listener-class>flex.messaging.HttpFlexSession
      </listener-class>
  </listener>
  <!-- MessageBroker Servlet -->
  <servlet>
      <servlet-name>MessageBrokerServlet</servlet-name>
      <display-name>MessageBrokerServlet</display-name>
      <servlet-class>flex.messaging.MessageBrokerServlet
      </servlet-class>
      <init-param>
          <param-name>services.configuration.file
          </param-name>
          <param-value>/WEB-INF/flex/services-config.xml
          </param-value>
      </init-param>
      <load-on-startup>1</load-on-startup>
  </servlet>
  <servlet-mapping>
```

```
    <servlet-name>MessageBrokerServlet</servlet-name>
    <url-pattern>/messagebroker/*</url-pattern>>
</servlet-mapping>
```

The other servlet mapping you see in the *web.xml* file is for the
RDSDispatchServlet, which Flash Builder uses to create a data
service by introspecting server-side classes.

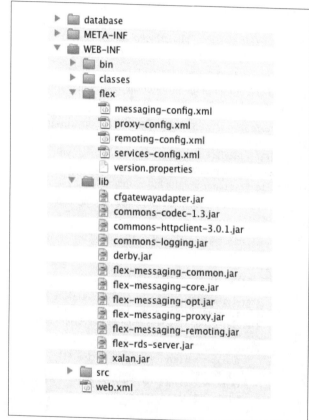

Figure 4-7. Locate the required BlazeDS files

Step 2: Open the services-config.xml and remoting-config.xml files

These files are located in the */testdrive/WEB-INF/flex/* folder.

In the *services-config.xml* file, you will see the following include statement for *remoting-config.xml*:

```
<service-include file-path="remoting-config.xml" />
```

In *remoting-config.xml*, locate the following code, which specifies the employeeService destination:

```
<destination id="employeeService">
    <properties>
        <source>services.EmployeeService</source>
        <scope>application</scope>
    </properties>
</destination>
```

The application on the production server that you add your application to must also have a *remoting-config.xml* with a destination with this name and that points to the correct Java class. The Java class can be located in a different place than it was on the development server; this destination must reflect the location on the production server.

Step 3: Locate the Flex application's reference to the services-config.xml file

In Flash Builder, select Project→Properties and select Flex Compiler. You will see a compiler argument that looks like the following:

```
-services "/Applications/tomcat/webapps/testdrive/WEB-INF/
          flex/services-config.xml"
```

This compiler argument was added when you created the project (as a J2EE project using BlazeDS).

Step 4: In Flash Builder, browse the generated EmployeeService file

This is the *services.employeeservice._Super_EmployeeService.as* file. Locate the destination assignment statement (Figure 4-8).

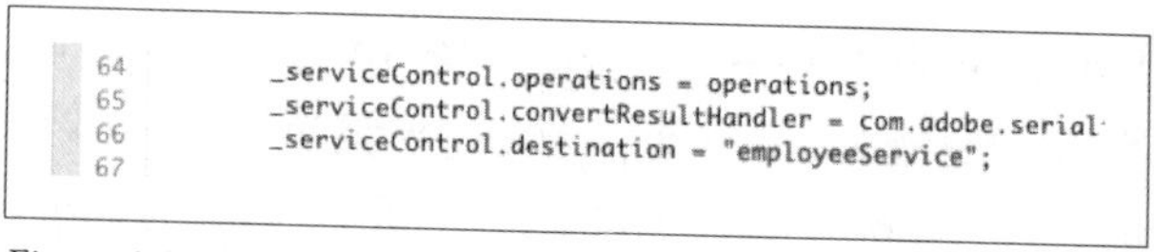

```
64          _serviceControl.operations = operations;
65          _serviceControl.convertResultHandler = com.adobe.serial·
66          _serviceControl.destination = "employeeService";
67
```

Figure 4-8. Locate the code specifying the destination for the Java class

When you create a data service in Flash Builder, you select a service from a list of destinations already defined in the *remoting-config.xml* file.

If the class ever changes, you can refresh the data service from the Data/Services view to update the generated files. If you move the class, make sure the destination in the *remoting-config.xml* file is updated to reflect the new location. If you rename the class during development, though, you will need to re-create the data service.

Congratulations! You've learned the basics for deploying a Flex application: creating a release version, including the application on a web page, and ensuring your application can access your server-side service files.

Change the Appearance of Your Application

In the previous chapters, you learned to create, debug, and deploy a Flex application. In this chapter, you will learn how to change the appearance of your application using styling and skinning; you will learn to create a stylesheet and define style rules that you apply to your application.

Use Styling

With styling, you set component styles inline in MXML (as you already have) or preferably, in a stylesheet using selectors (style rules). Each component has a limited number of defined styles. For example, you can set styles for a label, including font-size, font-family, and color. For a button, you can also set a corner-radius style. If you want to change the appearance of a component more drastically than is possible with a component's styles, you need to create or edit the associated component skin—the file specifying what the component should look like.

The Flex framework includes two families of components: Spark and MX. The tags that start with s (for example, <s:Button>) are new Flex 4 Spark components. The tags that start with mx (for example, `<mx:DataGrid>`) are the older Flex components. You set the appearance of MX components primarily using styling. The new Spark components have been rearchitected to primarily use a skinning (rather than styling) model in which each component's associated skin file manages everything related to a component's appearance, including its graphics, its layout, and its states.

Step 1: Create a Stylesheet and a CSS Global Selector

In Design mode with any object selected, navigate to the Appearance view and change font and color styles (Figure 5-1).

If you don't want to choose your own values, here are some you can use: `font-family: Verdana`, `font-size: 10`, `chrome-color: #7F7364`, `selection-color: #BFB59F`, `rollover-color: #E5DFC3`, `focus-color: #7F7364`.

The components in the design area will reflect these new styles. Even though the global font size is set to 10 pixels, the XYZ Label is still large because it has a `font-size` style set inline in its MXML tag.

Switch to Source mode. You will see the following new `Style` tag below the `Application` tag:

```
<fx:Style source="TestDrive.css"/>
```

In the Package Explorer, you will see a new file, *Test-Drive.css*. Open this file. You will see the following global CSS selector, whose styles will be applied to all components:

```
/* CSS file */
@namespace s "library://ns.adobe.com/flex/spark";
@namespace mx "library://ns.adobe.com/flex/mx";
global
{
    font-family: Verdana;
    font-size: 10;
    chrome-color: #7F7364;
    selection-color: #BFB59F;
    roll-over-color: #E5DFC3;
    focus-color: #7F7364;
}
```

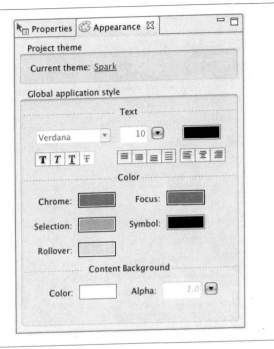

Figure 5-1. Set global styles in the Appearance view

Run the application to see the different colors for component chrome, rollover, selection, and focus (Figure 5-2).

Step 2: Create a CSS Type Selector

In Design mode, select one of the buttons and change its radius to 5 in the Properties view. Click the Convert to CSS button. In the New Style Rule dialog box (Figure 5-3), select "Specific component."

A CSS type selector is created with styles that will automatically be applied to all component instances of this type—in this case, all buttons.

Figure 5-2. View the different component colors

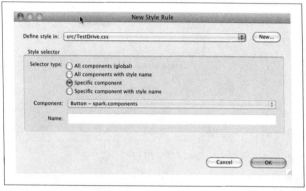

Figure 5-3. Create a CSS type selector

Return to *TestDrive.css*. You will see the following new CSS type selector:

```
s|Button
{
    cornerRadius: 5;
}
```

The **s** in front of **Button** specifies that this is the style for Spark buttons, not MX buttons. Return to *TestDrive.mxml* in Design mode or run the application. All the buttons now have rounded corners.

Step 3: Modify a CSS Selector

In *TestDrive.css*, add the color white (#FFFFFF) and the font weight bold to the button selector.

When typing styles, press Ctrl-space bar to force Content Assist to pop up so you can select styles from this list (Figure 5-4).

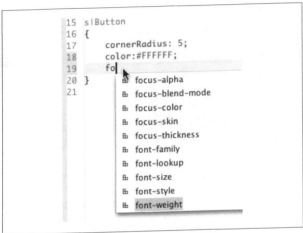

Figure 5-4. Use Content Assist when editing stylesheets

Return to *TestDrive.mxml* in Design mode or run the application. All the buttons now have bold white text, but it is difficult to read a disabled button (Figure 5-5).

Figure 5-5. Buttons as displayed in Design mode

Step 4: Create a CSS Pseudoselector

In *TestDrive.css*, add the following code to create a pseudoselector for the button's disabled state and set its color to black, #000000:

```
s|Button:disabled
{
    color:#000000;
}
```

Look at a component's API to find its defined skin states (Figure 5-6). Remember, you can open a component's API by selecting Help→Dynamic Help, clicking a tag in MXML, then clicking the API link in the Help view.

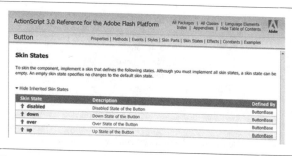

Figure 5-6. Locate the states of a Button component in its API

Return to *TestDrive.mxml* in Design mode or run the application. You will now be able to read a disabled button (Figure 5-7).

Figure 5-7. Disabled buttons are now readable

Step 5: Create a CSS Class Selector

In Design mode, select the Departments button and change its font size to 12 in the Properties view. Click the Convert to CSS button. In the New Style Rule dialog box (Figure 5-8), select "All components with style name" and name the style navButton.

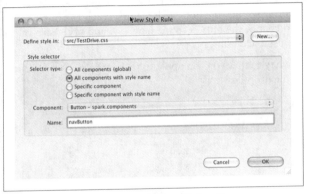

Figure 5-8. Create a CSS class selector called navButton

Return to *TestDrive.css*. You will see the following new CSS class selector, which you can selectively apply to any component:

```
.navButton
{
    fontSize: 12;
}
```

Return to Source mode in *TestDrive.mxml* and locate the deptBtn button. It now has a styleName property (for one state) set equal to the name of the class selector you just defined:

```
<s:Button x="124" y="85" label="Departments" id="deptBtn"
    enabled.Departments="false"
    click="deptBtn_clickHandler(event)"
    styleName.Employees="navButton"/>
```

Use the following to apply this property to all states:

```
styleName="navButton"
```

Step 6: Assign a CSS Class Selector to Another Component

In Design mode, select the Employees button and select the navButton style in the Properties view (Figure 5-9). Move the buttons so they are not overlapping. Switch to Source mode and change the button so the new x, y, and styleName values are used in all states.

Any styles that you can apply to that component will appear in the drop-down list.

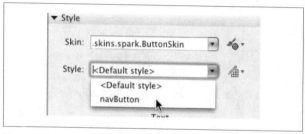

Figure 5-9. Assign a CSS class selector to a component

The Button tags should appear as follows:

```
<s:Button x="36" y="85" label="Employees" id="empBtn"
  enabled="false"
  styleName="navButton" enabled.Departments="true"/>
<s:Button label="Departments" id="deptBtn"
  click="deptBtn_clickHandler(event)"
  styleName="navButton" x="138" y="85"
  enabled.Departments="false"/>
```

Both of the buttons now have larger text than the other buttons—you selectively applied the navButton style to these two buttons.

Step 7: Style the DataGrid

In *TestDrive.css*, add a type selector for the mx|DataGrid and set its alternating-item-colors to #F8F8F4, #FFFFFF and its header-style-name to titles. Create a class selector called titles with a color of white and a font-weight of bold.

Your selectors should appear as follows:

```
mx|DataGrid
{
    alternating-item-colors:#F8F8F4,#FFFFFF;
    header-style-name:titles;
}
.titles{
    color:#FFFFFF;
    font-weight:bold;
}
```

Return to *TestDrive.mxml* in Design mode or run the application. The DataGrid header text and rows should now be styled as shown in Figure 5-10.

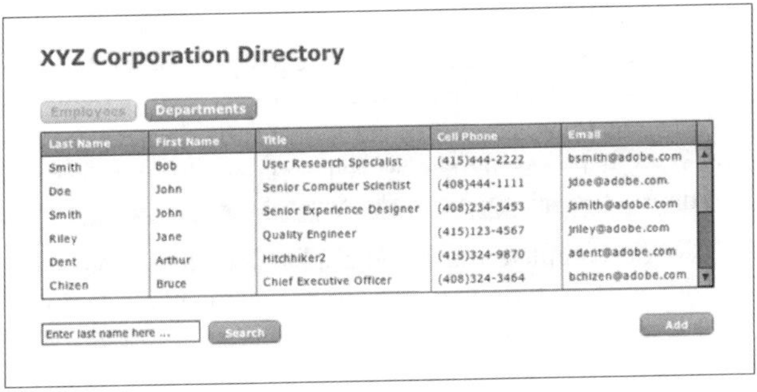

Figure 5-10. The new DataGrid styles

Step 8: Create a CSS ID Selector

In Source mode, give the XYZ Label an ID of xyz and remove its color, fontWeight, and fontSize styles. In *TestDrive.css*, create an ID selector for the Label using #xyz and set the color to #403029, the font-weight to bold, and the font-size to 20.

Your label should appear as follows:

```
<s:Label id="xyz" x="36" y="36"
   text="XYZ Corporation Directory"/>
```

Your CSS ID selector should appear as follows:

```
#xyz
{
    color: #403029;
    fontSize: 20;
    fontWeight: bold;
}
```

Return to *TestDrive.mxml* in Design mode or run the application and make sure the XYZ label is large, brown, and bold.

Step 9: Set the Application Background Color

In the Application tag, set the backgroundColor style to a new color (#F9F8E9). Run the application—it should appear styled as shown in Figure 5-11.

In this section, you learned to create a stylesheet and define CSS global, type, class, pseudo, and ID selectors that you applied to your application. In addition to these selectors, you can also create component-specific class selectors and descendant selectors.

When you complete the styled application steps, your code should look like the following (you can download the complete sample application at *www.adobe.com/devnet/flex/testdrive/assets/testdrive_style_skin.zip*):

TestDrive.mxml

```
<?xml version="1.0" encoding="utf-8"?>
<s:Application ... backgroundColor="#F9F8E9">
    <fx:Style source="TestDrive.css"/>
(...)
</s:Application>
```

TestDrive.css

```css
/* CSS file */
@namespace s  "library://ns.adobe.com/flex/spark";
@namespace mx "library://ns.adobe.com/flex/mx";

global
{
    font-family: Verdana;
    font-size: 10;
    chrome-color: #7F7364;
    selection-color: #BFB59F;
    roll-over-color: #E5DFC3;
    focus-color: #7F7364;
}
s|Button
{
    cornerRadius: 5;
    color:#FFFFFF;
    font-weight:bold;
}
s|Button:disabled{

    color:#000000;
}
.navButton
{
    fontSize: 12;
}
mx|DataGrid
{
    alternating-item-colors:#F8F8F4,#FFFFFF;
    header-style-name:titles;
}
.titles{
    color:#FFFFFF;
    font-weight:bold;
}
#xyz
{
    color: #403029;
    fontSize: 20;
    fontWeight: bold;
}
```

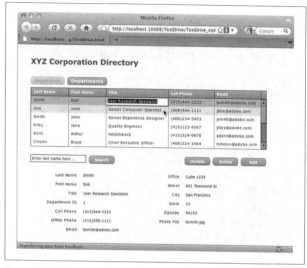

Figure 5-11. The completed styled application

Add Components to Skins

In this section, you will create a button that has both text and an icon on it. To accomplish this, you will create a new button skin based on the default button skin and then modify its layout and add a new BitmapImage component to it.

Step 1: Create a New Button Skin File

In Design mode, select the Chart data button in the Departments state and, in the Properties view, click the button next to the Skin field and select Create Skin (Figure 5-12). In the New MXML Skin dialog box, name it ChartButtonSkin and leave the defaults selected (Figure 5-13).

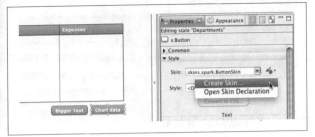

Figure 5-12. Create a new skin for the Chart data button

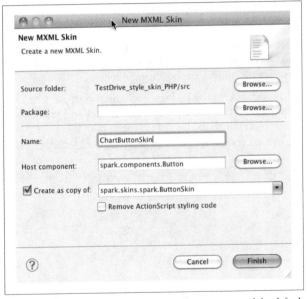

Figure 5-13. Create a new ChartButtonSkin as a copy of the default ButtonSkin

In *TestDrive.mxml*, switch to Source mode and look at the Chart data button. It now has a `skinClass` style set to the name of the new skin ChartButtonSkin, which right now is the same as the default skin (you can also set this style in the stylesheet):

```
<s:Button includeIn="Departments" x="609" y="293"
    label="Chart data" skinClass="ChartButtonSkin"/>
```

Step 2: Review the Skin Class

In *ChartButtonSkin.mxml*, switch to Source mode and review the code (Figure 5-14). The host component specifies which component this skin can be applied to:

```
[HostComponent("spark.components.Button")]
```

Next, there are several functions that adjust the graphics based on any style values you set, followed by the states. These match those for the button, the host component.

Below this are graphics tags, including multiple Rect and LinearGradient tags, which draw rectangles and gradients—the graphics for all the buttons in the application.

```
 92      <!-- layer 1: shadow -->
 93      <!--- @private -->
 94      <s:Rect id="shadow" left="-1" right="-1" top="-1" bottom="-1" radiusX="2">
 95          <s:fill>
 96              <s:LinearGradient rotation="90">
 97                  <s:GradientEntry color="0x000000"
 98                                   color.down="0xFFFFFF"
 99                                   alpha="0.01"
100                                   alpha.down="0" />
101                  <s:GradientEntry color="0x000000"
102                                   color.down="0xFFFFFF"
103                                   alpha="0.07"
104                                   alpha.down="0.5" />
105              </s:LinearGradient>
106          </s:fill>
107      </s:Rect>
108
109      <!-- layer 2: fill -->
110      <!--- @private -->
111      <s:Rect id="fill" left="1" right="1" top="1" bottom="1" radiusX="2">
112          <s:fill>
113              <s:LinearGradient rotation="90">
114                  <s:GradientEntry color="0xFFFFFF"
115                                   color.over="0xBBBDBD"
```

Figure 5-14. Review the graphics code

Finally, at the end you will see a Label control. This is the component whose text property is set when you set a button's label property. It is called a *skin part*. The various attributes specify where the label should appear on the button:

```
<s:Label id="labelDisplay"
              textAlign="center"
              verticalAlign="middle"
              maxDisplayedLines="1"
              horizontalCenter="0" verticalCenter="1"
              left="10" right="10" top="2" bottom="2">
      </s:Label>
```

Step 3: Place the Label Inside a Group Container with HorizontalLayout

Set the layout property of the Group component to an instance of the HorizontalLayout class. Move the label inside the group and transfer the layout properties from the Label control to either the group or HorizontalLayout as appropriate.

Here, you are creating a group with a HorizontalLayout to have a label and an icon next to each other (horizontally) on the button.

Your code should appear as follows:

```
<s:Group horizontalCenter="0" verticalCenter="1"
left="10" right="10" top="2" bottom="2" >
      <s:layout>
          <s:HorizontalLayout verticalAlign="middle"/>
      </s:layout>
      <s:Label id="labelDisplay" textAlign="center"
          maxDisplayedLines="1"/>
</s:Group>
```

Run the application or switch to Design mode for *Test-Drive.mxml*. The Chart data button should look exactly the same as it did before; you haven't changed it yet.

Step 4: Add a BitmapImage Component

Inside the group, add a BitmapImage component and set its source property to an embedded image (*pieIcon.gif*) in your project folder.

You can use your own image or the one supplied with the Test Drive files. To use your own image, simply copy it into your project *src* folder and then reference it. To use the Test Drive icon, copy the *pieIcon.gif* file located in the sample files for this module at *www.adobe.com/devnet/flex/testdrive/assets/test drive_style_skin.zip* and paste it into your project *src* folder.

Your code should appear as follows:

```
<s:Group horizontalCenter="0" verticalCenter="1" left="10"
  right="10" top="2" bottom="2" >
   <s:layout>
      <s:HorizontalLayout verticalAlign="middle"/>
   </s:layout>
   <s:Label id="labelDisplay" textAlign="center"
     maxDisplayedLines="1"/>
   <s:BitmapImage source="@Embed('pieIcon.gif')"/>
</s:Group>
```

Save the file. Switch to Design mode for *TestDrive.mxml*. You will see the icon on your button (Figure 5-15). Move the buttons so they are not overlapping.

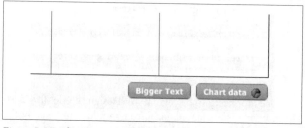

Figure 5-15. The new icon on the Chart data button

In this section, you learned to change the appearance of a component by extending a default component skin and adding additional components to it. Your code should look like the following (you can download the complete sample application at *www.adobe.com/devnet/flex/testdrive/assets/test drive_style_skin.zip*):

TestDrive.mxml

```
<?xml version="1.0" encoding="utf-8"?>
  <s:Application ... >
      (...)
      <s:Button label="Chart data"
        skinClass="ChartButtonSkin" .../>
      (...)
  </s:Application>
```

ChartButtonSkin.mxml

```
<?xml version="1.0" encoding="utf-8"?>
<s:SparkSkin xmlns:fx="http://ns.adobe.com/mxml/2009"
    xmlns:s="library://ns.adobe.com/flex/spark"
    xmlns:fb="http://ns.adobe.com/flashbuilder/2009"
    minWidth="21" minHeight="21" alpha.disabled="0.5">
    <fx:Metadata>
        <![CDATA[
        [HostComponent("spark.components.Button")]
        ]]>
    </fx:Metadata>

    <fx:Script fb:purpose="styling">
        <![CDATA[
            static private const
              exclusions:Array = ["labelDisplay"];
            override public function get
              colorizeExclusions():Array
              {return exclusions;}
            override protected function
              initializationComplete():void { (...) }
            override protected function
              updateDisplayList(unscaledWidth:Number,
              unscaledHeight:Number) : void
            { (...) }
            private var cornerRadius:Number = 2;
        ]]>
    </fx:Script>
    <s:states>
        <s:State name="up" />
        <s:State name="over" />
        <s:State name="down" />
```

```
        <s:State name="disabled" />
    </s:states>
    <!-- layer 1: shadow -->
    <s:Rect id="shadow" left="-1" right="-1" top="-1"
      bottom="-1" radiusX="2">
        <s:fill>
            <s:LinearGradient rotation="90">
                <s:GradientEntry color="0x000000"
                                 color.down="0xFFFFFF"
                                 alpha="0.01"
                                 alpha.down="0" />
                <s:GradientEntry color="0x000000"
                                 color.down="0xFFFFFF"
                                 alpha="0.07"
                                 alpha.down="0.5" />
            </s:LinearGradient>
        </s:fill>
    </s:Rect>
    <!-- layer 2: fill -->
    <s:Rect id="fill" ... />
    <!-- layer 3: fill lowlight -->
    <s:Rect id="lowlight".../>
    <!-- layer 4: fill highlight -->
    <s:Rect id="highlight" .../>
    <!-- layer 5: highlight stroke (all states except
    down) -->
    <s:Rect id="highlightStroke" .../>
    <!-- layer 6: highlight stroke (down state only) -->
    <s:Rect id="hldownstroke1" .../>
    <!-- layer 7: border - put on top of the fill so
    it doesn't disappear when scale is less than 1 -->
    <s:Rect id="border" .../>

    <!-- layer 8: text -->
    <s:Group horizontalCenter="0" verticalCenter="1"
      left="10" right="10" top="2" bottom="2" >
        <s:layout>
            <s:HorizontalLayout verticalAlign="middle"/>
        </s:layout>
        <s:Label id="labelDisplay" textAlign="center"
          maxDisplayedLines="1"/>
        <s:BitmapImage source="@Embed('pieIcon.gif')"/>
    </s:Group>
</s:SparkSkin>
```

Create Skins with New Graphics

In this section, you will create a component skin that has entirely new graphics and does not use the graphics code from a parent skin.

Step 1: Create a New Button Skin File

In Design mode, select the Bigger Text button in the Departments state and, in the Properties view, click the button next to the Skin field and select Create Skin. In the New MXML Skin dialog box, name it BiggerButtonSkin and uncheck "Create as copy of" (Figure 5-16).

Figure 5-16. Create a new BiggerButtonSkin as a new MXML skin

Step 2: Review the Skin Class

In *BiggerButtonSkin.mxml*, switch to Source mode and review the code. Because you specified the Host component to be a button, the HostComponent and states are already set:

```
<s:Skin xmlns:fx=http://ns.adobe.com/mxml/2009...>
    <!-- host component -->
    <fx:Metadata>
        [HostComponent("spark.components.Button")]
    </fx:Metadata>
    <!-- states -->
    <s:states>
        <s:State name="disabled" />
        <s:State name="down" />
        <s:State name="over" />
        <s:State name="up" />
    </s:states>
</s:Skin>
```

Step 3: Review the Graphics Code

Copy the *BiggerButton.fxg* file located in the sample files for this module (*www.adobe.com/devnet/flex/testdrive/assets/test drive_style_skin.zip*). Paste *BiggerButton.fxg* into your project *src* folder. Open the file.

This file was drawn in Fireworks and then exported by selecting Commands→Export to FXG. You can also create FXG files using Illustrator or Photoshop.

In the FXG file, you will see code for creating graphics (Figure 5-17). You can copy and paste this code into your BiggerButtonSkin class or just reference it as we will do next.

Step 4: Add the Graphics to the Skin

After the states in *BiggerButtonSkin.mxml*, use Code Assist to add an instance of the BiggerButton FXG class (Figure 5-18).

Because you used Code Assist, the namespace assignment (xmlns:local="*") was written for you.

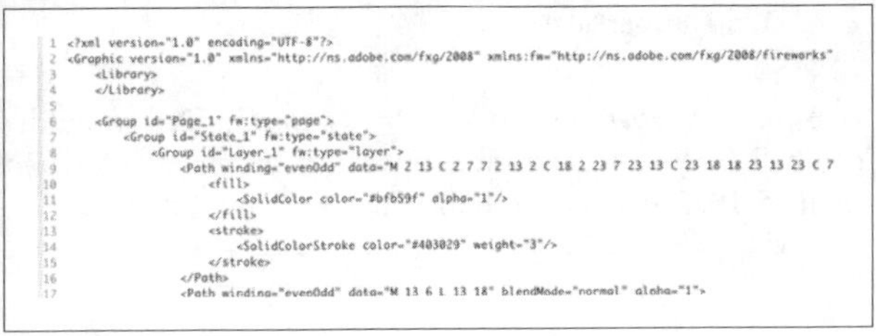

Figure 5-17. Review the graphics code in BiggerButton.fxg

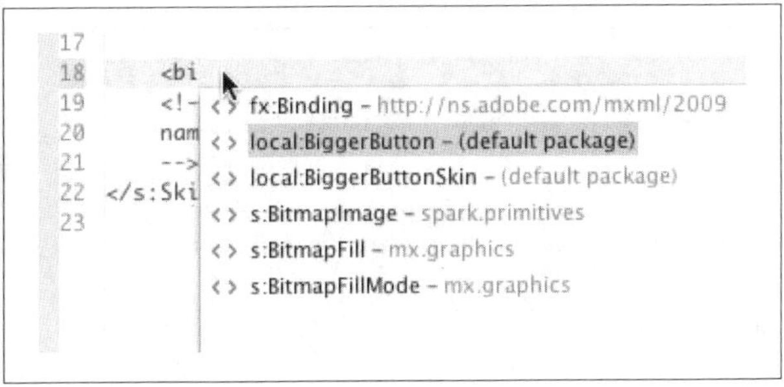

Figure 5-18. Add the BiggerButton FXG class

This tells the compiler where to find this class. Put the FXG file in the same folder as the MXML file (the default package), so * specifies to look for files in the same folder.

Your skin class should appear as follows:

```
<?xml version="1.0" encoding="utf-8"?>
<s:Skin xmlns:fx="http://ns.adobe.com/mxml/2009"
  xmlns:s="library://ns.adobe.com/flex/spark"
  xmlns:mx="library://ns.adobe.com/flex/mx"
  xmlns:local="*">
  <fx:Metadata>
      [HostComponent("spark.components.Button")]
  </fx:Metadata>
  <s:states>
      <s:State name="disabled" />
      <s:State name="down" />
      <s:State name="over" />
      <s:State name="up" />
  </s:states>
```

```
        <local:BiggerButton/>
    </s:Skin>
```

Save the file and return to *TestDrive.mxml* in Design mode. You will see the Bigger button with the new skin, as shown in Figure 5-19. Move it next to the Chart data button.

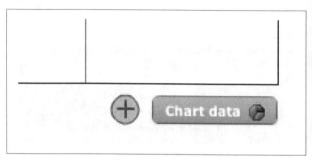

Figure 5-19. The new graphics for the Bigger button

Run the application. Click the Departments button and then the Bigger button. The DataGrid text will get larger (Figure 5-20); the button works exactly as before—it just has a new look.

XYZ Corporation Directory

Name	ID	Manager	Budget	Expenses
User Experience	1	Big Boss	395000	412000
Engineering	2	Bill Lumburg	434000	436000
Space Exploration	3	Zaphod Beeblebrc	1625000	1833000
Corporate	4	Bruce Chizen	1130000	1500000
Advanced Physics	5	Albert Einstein	440000	444000

Figure 5-20. When you click the Bigger button, DataGrid text appears larger

Congratulations! In this chapter, you learned to change the appearance of your application using styling and skinning.

Your code should look like the following (download the complete sample application at *www.adobe.com/devnet/flex/test drive/assets/testdrive_style_skin.zip*):

TestDrive.mxml

```
<?xml version="1.0" encoding="utf-8"?>
  <s:Application ... >
      (...)
  <s:Button id="biggerBtn"
    skinClass="BiggerButtonSkin" .../>
      (...)
  </s:Application>
```

BiggerButtonSkin.mxml

```
<?xml version="1.0" encoding="utf-8"?>
<s:Skin xmlns:fx="http://ns.adobe.com/mxml/2009"
  xmlns:s="library://ns.adobe.com/flex/spark"
  xmlns:mx="library://ns.adobe.com/flex/mx"
  xmlns:local="*">
    <fx:Metadata>
        [HostComponent("spark.components.Button")]
    </fx:Metadata>

    <s:states>
        <s:State name="disabled" />
        <s:State name="down" />
        <s:State name="over" />
        <s:State name="up" />
    </s:states>
    <local:BiggerButton/>
</s:Skin>
```

BiggerButton.fxg

```
<?xml version="1.0" encoding="UTF-8"?>
<Graphic version="1.0"
    xmlns="http://ns.adobe.com/fxg/2008"
    xmlns:fw="http://ns.adobe.com/fxg/2008/fireworks"
    viewHeight= "25" viewWidth= "25">
  <Library></Library>
  <Group id="Page_1" fw:type="page">
    <Group id="State_1" fw:type="state">
      <Group id="Layer_1" fw:type="layer">
        <Path winding="evenOdd" blendMode="normal"
        alpha="1">
          data="M 2 13 C 2 7 7 2 13 2 C 18 2 23 7 23 13
```

```
              C 23 18 18 23 13 23 C 7 23 2 18 2 13 Z "
    <fill>
      <SolidColor color="#bfb59f" alpha="1"/>
    </fill>
    <stroke>
      <SolidColorStroke color="#403029" weight="3"/>
    </stroke>
  </Path>
  <Path winding="evenOdd" data="M 13 6 L 13 18"
    blendMode="normal" alpha="1">
    <stroke>
      <SolidColorStroke color="#403029" weight="2"/>
    </stroke>
  </Path>
  <Path winding="evenOdd" data="M 7 12 L 19 12"
    blendMode="normal" alpha="1">
    <stroke>
      <SolidColorStroke color="#403029" weight="2"/>
    </stroke>
  </Path>
    </Group>
   </Group>
  </Group>
</Graphic>
```

CHAPTER 6

Add Charts and Graphs

In the previous chapter, you learned to build, debug, deploy, style, and skin a Flex application. In this chapter, you will add and format charts.

Add a Pie Chart

The following steps describe how to create and configure the data for a pie chart.

Step 1: Create a New State DepartmentChart with a Pie Chart

Disable the Chart data button and add a PieChart called `deptPieCht` from the Components view (Figure 6-1). Arrange the chart as shown in Figure 6-2.

Step 2: Specify the Data for the Chart

In Source mode, set the PieChart `dataProvider` to that for the DataGrid, `deptDg.dataProvider`. Set the PieSeries `field` to `budget` and its `nameField` to `name`. Remove the `displayName` property.

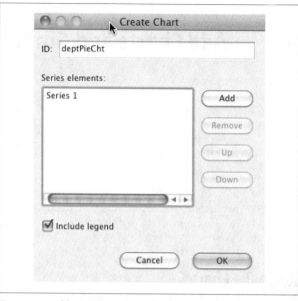

Figure 6-1. Add a PieChart component

The `field` is the property of the objects in the `dataProvider` to chart. The `nameField` is the property of the objects in the `dataProvider` to display in the legend.

Your code should appear as follows:

```
<mx:PieChart includeIn="DepartmentChart" x="35" y="308"
  id="deptPieCht"
  width="282" height="282"
  dataProvider="{deptDg.dataProvider}">
    <mx:series>
        <mx:PieSeries field="budget" nameField="name"/>
    </mx:series>
</mx:PieChart>
<mx:Legend includeIn="DepartmentChart"
  dataProvider="{deptPieCht}"
  x="323" y="308"/>
```

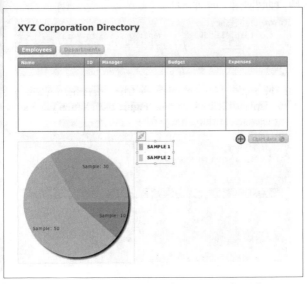

Figure 6-2. Arrange the DepartmentChart state as shown here

Step 3: Configure Your Application Such That States Are Switched When the Chart Data Button Is Clicked

Assign the Chart data button an `id` of `chartBtn` and generate a `click` handler for it. Make it the `click` handler for all states. Inside the handler, set the `currentState` to `DepartmentChart`.

Delete the state associated with the `click` event in either Source mode or Design mode, right-click the button, and select Apply Current Properties to All States. Your code for the button should appear as follows:

```
<s:Button id="chartBtn"
includeIn="DepartmentChart,DepartmentDetails,Departments"
x="591" y="293" label="Chart data"
skinClass="ChartButtonSkin" enabled.DepartmentChart="false"
enabled.DepartmentDetails="false"
click="chartBtn_clickHandler(event)" />
```

The handler should appear as follows:

```
protected function
  chartBtn_clickHandler(event:MouseEvent):void
{
  currentState="DepartmentChart";
}
```

Run the application and click the Chart data button. The pie chart displays the budget data (Figure 6-3). When you mouse over the chart, nothing happens.

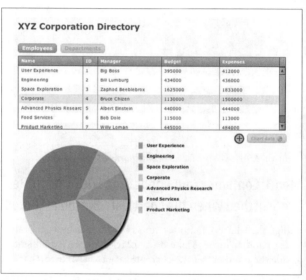

Figure 6-3. Display the department budget data in a pie chart

Step 4: Display Chart Labels and Data Tips

Set the PieChart showDataTips property to true. Set the PieSeries labelField property to name and the labelPosition style to inside.

The `labelField` is the property of the objects in the `dataProvider` to display on the PieChart. You have to set the `labelPosition` to inside, outside, callout, or insideWithCallout to specify where the labels should appear; the default value is none.

Your code should appear as follows:

```
<mx:PieChart includeIn="DepartmentChart" x="35" y="308"
  id="deptPieCht"
  width="282" height="282"
  dataProvider="{deptDg.dataProvider}"
  showDataTips="true">
    <mx:series>
        <mx:PieSeries field="budget" nameField="name"
          labelField="name"
          labelPosition="inside"/>
    </mx:series>
</mx:PieChart>
```

Run the application. You will see labels on the chart, and when you mouse over a slice you will see a data tip, as shown in Figure 6-4.

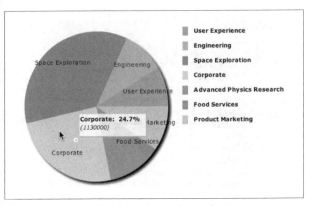

Figure 6-4. Add labels and data tips to the pie chart

Step 5: Delete the Legend

You no longer need the legend, because you have added labels. To delete the legend, delete the Legend component in Design mode or delete the Legend tag in Source mode.

Your final code should look like the following (you can download the complete sample application at *www.adobe.com/dev net/flex/testdrive/assets/testdrive_add_charts.zip*):

```
<?xml version="1.0" encoding="utf-8"?>
<s:Application ...>
    <fx:Script>
        <![CDATA[
            (...)
            protected function
              chartBtn_clickHandler(event:MouseEvent):void
            {
              currentState="DepartmentChart";
            }
        ]]>
    </fx:Script>
    <s:states>
        (...)
        <s:State name="DepartmentChart"/>
    </s:states>
    (...)
    <s:Buttonid="empBtn"
      click.DepartmentChart=
        "empBtn_clickHandler(event)" .../>
    <s:Button id="deptBtn"
      enabled.DepartmentChart="false" .../>
    <mx:DataGrid id="deptDg"
      includeIn="DepartmentChart,Departments" .../>
    <s:Button id="chartBtn"
      includeIn="DepartmentChart,Departments"
      enabled.DepartmentChart="false"
      click="chartBtn_clickHandler(event)".../>
    <s:Button id="biggerBtn"
      includeIn="DepartmentChart,Departments" .../>
    <mx:PieChart includeIn="DepartmentChart" x="35"
      y="308" id="deptPieCht" width="282" height="282"
      dataProvider="{deptDg.dataProvider}"
      showDataTips="true">
        <mx:series>
            <mx:PieSeries field="budget" nameField="name"
```

```
            labelField="name"
            labelPosition="inside"/>
    </mx:series>
</mx:PieChart>
<!--<mx:Legend includeIn="DepartmentChart"
dataProvider="{deptPieCht}"
x="323" y="308"/>-->
</s:Application>
```

Add a Column Chart

In this section, you will display data in a column chart. The column chart will be displayed when the user clicks a pie chart item, and it will show detailed data for the selected item.

Step 1: Create a New State, DepartmentDetails, with a Column Chart

Add a ColumnChart from the Components view called deptColCht. Arrange the chart as shown in Figure 6-5.

Step 2: Configure Your Application Such That States Are Switched When a Department Slice Is Clicked on the Pie Chart

Add an itemClick handler to the PieChart, and inside the handler set the currentState to DepartmentDetails.

Your opening PieChart tag should appear as follows:

```
<mx:PieChart includeIn="DepartmentChart,DepartmentDetails"
    x="35" y="308" id="deptPieCht" width="282" height="282"
    dataProvider="{deptDg.dataProvider}" showDataTips="true"
    itemClick="deptPieCht_itemClickHandler(event)">
```

The handler code should appear as follows:

```
protected function
  deptPieCht_itemClickHandler(event:ChartItemEvent):void
{
```

```
        currentState="DepartmentDetails";
    }
```

If you did not generate the event handler automatically, be sure to select **ChartItemEvent** from Code Assist so the following **import** statement is written for you:

```
import mx.charts.events.ChartItemEvent;
```

Run the application and click an item in the pie chart. You will see a column chart with no data displayed.

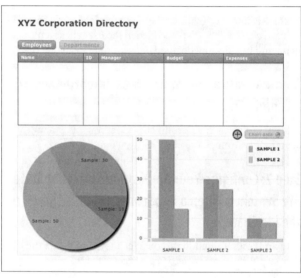

Figure 6-5. Arrange the DepartmentDetails state as shown here

Step 3: Create the ColumnChart dataProvider

Inside the PieChart **itemClick** handler, set the ColumnChart **dataProvider** equal to the array of objects returned by the function below.

Copy and paste the following `createDataProvider()` function into your `Script` block. It creates an array of objects with properties called `field`, `actual`, and `est` for each of the items in a department's budget and expense data:

```
private function createDataProvider(item:Object):Array
{
  var dp:Array=
    [{field:'salaries',actual:item.actualsalary,
      est:item.estsalary},
     {field:'travel',actual:item.actualtravel,
      est:item.esttravel},
     {field:'supplies',actual:item.actualtravel,
      est:item.esttravel},
     {field:'contractors',actual:item.actualcontractors,
      est:item.estcontractors}];
  return dp;
}
```

Call this function inside the PieChart `itemClick` handler and pass it the selected item in the PieChart, which you get from the event object, `event.hitData.item`. Set the ColumnChart `dataProvider` equal to the array of objects returned by this function. Your code should appear as follows:

```
protected function
  deptPieCht_itemClickHandler(event:ChartItemEvent):void
{
  currentState="DepartmentDetails";
  deptColCht.dataProvider=
    createDataProvider(event.hitData.item);
}
```

Step 4: Specify the Data to Chart

Set the ColumnSeries `yField` to `est` and its `displayName` to `Estimated`.

The ColumnChart code should appear as follows:

```
<mx:ColumnChart includeIn="DepartmentDetails" x="325"
  y="308" id="deptColCht" height="278" width="363">
  <mx:series>
    <mx:ColumnSeries displayName="Estimated"
      yField="est"/>
  </mx:series>
```

```
    </mx:ColumnChart>
    <mx:Legend includeIn="DepartmentDetails"
      dataProvider="{deptColCht}" x="596" y="325"/>
```

Run the application. When you click an item in the pie chart,
you will see details for that department in the column chart
(Figure 6-6).

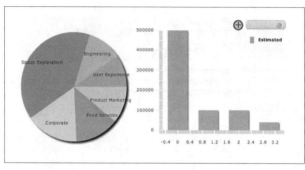

Figure 6-6. Show department expense data in a column chart

Step 5: Specify Axis Types and Titles

Set the ColumnChart horizontalAxis property to an instance
of the CategoryAxis class with a categoryField of field and a
title of Expenses. Set the ColumnChart verticalAxis property
to an instance of the LinearAxis class with a minimum of 0, a
maximum of 500000, and a title of Amount.

The ColumnChart code should appear as follows:

```
    <mx:ColumnChart includeIn="DepartmentDetails" x="325"
      y="308" id="deptColCht" height="278" width="363">
      <mx:horizontalAxis>
        <mx:CategoryAxis title="Expenses"
          categoryField="field"/>
      </mx:horizontalAxis>
      <mx:verticalAxis>
        <mx:LinearAxis title="Amount" minimum="0"
          maximum="500000"/>
      </mx:verticalAxis>
      <mx:series>
```

```
      <mx:ColumnSeries  displayName="Estimated"
        yField="est"/>
    </mx:series>
  </mx:ColumnChart>
```

Run the application. You will see the names of the fields displayed on the horizontal axis and titles for both axes, as shown in Figure 6-7.

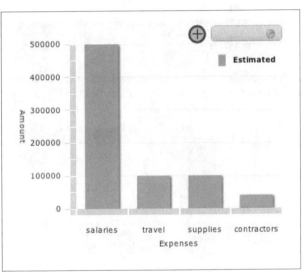

Figure 6-7. Specify axis types and titles

Step 6: Add a Second Series and Show Data Tips

Add a second `ColumnSeries` tag to the ColumnChart `series` property and set its `yField` to `actual` and its `displayName` to `Actual`. Set the ColumnChart `showDataTips` property to `true`.

The code should appear as follows:

```
<mx:ColumnChart includeIn="DepartmentDetails" x="325"
  y="308" id="deptColCht" height="278" width="363"
  showDataTips="true">
    <mx:horizontalAxis>
```

```
    <mx:CategoryAxis title="Expenses"
      categoryField="field"/>
  </mx:horizontalAxis>
  <mx:verticalAxis>
    <mx:LinearAxis title="Amount" minimum="0"
      maximum="1000000"/>
  </mx:verticalAxis>
  <mx:series>
    <mx:ColumnSeries  displayName="Estimated"
      yField="est"/>
    <mx:ColumnSeries  displayName="Actual"
      yField="actual"/>
  </mx:series>
</mx:ColumnChart>
```

Run the application. You will see two sets of data, a legend, and data tips when you mouse over the columns (Figure 6-8).

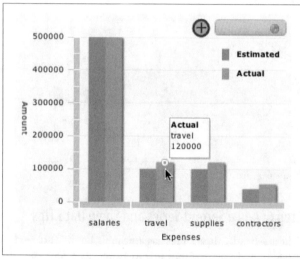

Figure 6-8. Add a second data series and data tips

Step 7: Display the Selected Department Name in the Axis Title

Assign the CategoryAxis an `id` of `expenseAxis` and inside the PieChart `itemClick` handler, set the `title` of this axis to the name of the selected item plus the string, `Expenses`.

The CategoryAxis code should appear as follows:

```
<mx:CategoryAxis id="expenseAxis" title="Expenses"
  categoryField="field"/>
```

The handler code should appear as follows:

```
protected function
  deptPieCht_itemClickHandler(event:ChartItemEvent):void
{
  currentState="DepartmentDetails";
  deptColCht.dataProvider=
    createDataProvider(event.hitData.item);
  expenseAxis.title=event.hitData.item.name+" Expenses";
}
```

Run the application and select different items in the pie chart. You will see the horizontal axis title change (Figure 6-9).

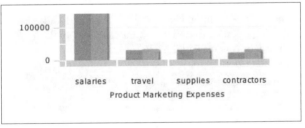

Figure 6-9. Display the selected department name in the axis title

Step 8: Animate the Data Change

In the Declarations block, create an instance of the SeriesIn
terpolate class called **interpolate** and set its **duration** property
to **1000**. To both of the ColumnSeries objects, add a new
attribute called **showDataEffect** and set it equal to the
interpolate object.

The **duration** property is set to a length of time in milliseconds.
Your new declaration code should appear as follows:

```
<fx:Declarations>
  (...)
  <mx:SeriesInterpolate id="interpolate" duration="1000"/>
</fx:Declarations>
```

The ColumnSeries objects should appear as follows:

```
<mx:ColumnSeries  displayName="Estimated" yField="est"
    showDataEffect="{interpolate}"/>
<mx:ColumnSeries  displayName="Actual" yField="actual"
    showDataEffect="{interpolate}"/>
```

Run the application and click different department slices in the
pie chart. Instead of instantly changing size, the columns now
grow larger or smaller as the underlying data changes.

After adding a column chart, your code should look like the
following (you can download the sample application at
*www.adobe.com/devnet/flex/testdrive/assets/test
drive_add_charts.zip*):

```
<?xml version="1.0" encoding="utf-8"?>
<s:Application ...>
  <fx:Script>
    <![CDATA[
      (...)
      import mx.charts.events.ChartItemEvent;

    protected function
      deptPieCht_itemClickHandler(
        event:ChartItemEvent):void
    {
      currentState="DepartmentDetails";
      deptColCht.dataProvider=
        createDataProvider(event.hitData.item);
```

```
      expenseAxis.title=event.hitData.item.name+
        " Expenses";
    }
      private function
        createDataProvider(item:Object):Array{
          var dp:Array= [{field:'salaries',
            actual:item.actualsalary,est:item.estsalary},
            {field:'travel',actual:item.actualtravel,
              est:item.esttravel},
            {field:'supplies',actual:item.actualtravel,
              est:item.esttravel},
            {field:'contractors',
              actual:item.actualcontractors,
              est:item.estcontractors}];
          return dp;
        }
  ]]>
</fx:Script>
<s:states>
    (...)
    <s:State name="DepartmentDetails"/>
</s:states>
<fx:Declarations>
    (...)
    <mx:SeriesInterpolate id="interpolate"
      duration="1000"/>
</fx:Declarations>
    (...)
<s:Button id="empBtn"
  click.DepartmentDetails=
    "empBtn_clickHandler(event)" .../>
<s:Button id="deptBtn"
  enabled.DepartmentDetails="false" .../>
<mx:DataGrid id="deptDg"
  includeIn="DepartmentChart,DepartmentDetails,
    Departments" .../>
<s:Button id="chartBtn"
  includeIn="DepartmentChart,DepartmentDetails,
    Departments"
  enabled.DepartmentDetails="false" .../>
<s:Button id="biggerBtn"
  includeIn="DepartmentChart,DepartmentDetails,
    Departments" .../>
  <mx:PieChart
    includeIn="DepartmentChart,DepartmentDetails"
    x="35" y="308" id="deptPieCht" width="282"
    height="282" dataProvider="{deptDg.dataProvider}"
```

```
      showDataTips="true"
      itemClick="deptPieCht_itemClickHandler(event)">
       <mx:series>
          <mx:PieSeries field="budget" nameField="name"
           labelField="name" labelPosition="inside" />
       </mx:series>
   </mx:PieChart>
   <mx:ColumnChart includeIn="DepartmentDetails" x="325"
      y="308" id="deptColCht" height="278" width="363"
      showDataTips="true">
      <mx:horizontalAxis>
         <mx:CategoryAxis id="expenseAxis" title="Expenses"
           categoryField="field"/>
      </mx:horizontalAxis>
      <mx:verticalAxis>
         <mx:LinearAxis title="Amount" minimum="0"
           maximum="500000"/>
      </mx:verticalAxis>
      <mx:series>
         <mx:ColumnSeries  displayName="Estimated"
           yField="est" showDataEffect="{interpolate}"/>
         <mx:ColumnSeries  displayName="Actual"
           yField="actual" showDataEffect="{interpolate}"/>
      </mx:series>
   </mx:ColumnChart>
   <mx:Legend includeIn="DepartmentDetails"
     dataProvider="{deptColCht}" x="596" y="325"/>
   <!--<mx:Legend includeIn="DepartmentChart"
     dataProvider="{deptPieCht}" x="323" y="308"/>-->
</s:Application>
```

Format Charts

In this tutorial, you will customize the pie and column charts.
You will change fill, axis, and tick colors; rotate axis titles; format axis titles and labels; and format data tips.

Step 1: Set Chart Fill Colors

In *TestDrive.css*, create a PieSeries type selector with the
fills style set to a list of at least seven
colors (#7F7364,#BFB59F,#E5DFC3,#586F99,#6782B2,#ADCAFF,
#F8F8F4). Create a class selector called brownFill with fill set

to brown (#403029). In *TestDrive.mxml*, set the styleName property of the Actual ColumnSeries to brownFill.

Your new selectors should appear as follows:

```
mx|PieSeries
{
  fills:#7F7364,#BFB59F,#E5DFC3,#586F99,#6782B2,#ADCAFF,
  #F8F8F4;
}
.brownFill
{
    fill:#403029;
}
```

The ColumnSeries should appear as follows:

```
<mx:ColumnSeries displayName="Actual" yField="actual"
  styleName="brownFill"/>
```

Run the application and drill down into department data. You will see your new colors in the pie and column chart (Figure 6-10).

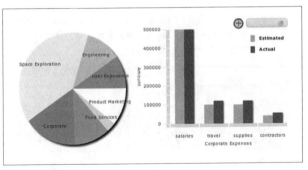

Figure 6-10. Customize the chart fill colors

Step 2: Set a Column Fill Color Dynamically

Assign the first ColumnSeries an id of estSeries and in the deptPieCht itemClick handler, use setStyle() to set the fill style to the color of the selected pie chart item: (event.hit Data.chartItem as PieSeriesItem).fill.

Your ColumnSeries code should appear as follows:

```
<mx:ColumnSeries id="estSeries" displayName="Estimated"
  yField="est" showDataEffect="{interpolate}"/>
```

Your handler code should appear as follows:

```
protected function
  deptPieCht_itemClickHandler(event:ChartItemEvent):void
{
  currentState="DepartmentDetails";
  deptColCht.dataProvider=
    createDataProvider(event.hitData.item);
  expenseAxis.title=event.hitData.item.name+" Expenses";
  estSeries.setStyle("fill",(event.hitData.chartItem
    as PieSeriesItem).fill);
}
```

Be sure to select PieSeriesItem from Code Assist so the following import statement is written for you:

```
import mx.charts.series.items.PieSeriesItem;
```

Run the application. When you select a department in the pie chart, the first series in the column chart is now the same color, as shown in Figure 6-11. Look at the position of the vertical axis title; you will flip this in the next step.

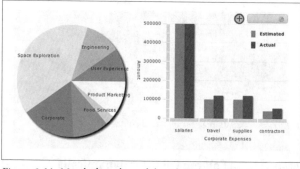

Figure 6-11. Match the colors of the selected pie chart item and the first column series

Step 3: Rotate the Axis Title

Set the LinearAxis `id` to `amountAxis` and set the ColumnChart `verticalAxisRenderers` property to an instance of the `AxisRenderer` class. For the AxisRenderer, set the `verticalAx isTitleAlignment` style to `vertical` and the `axis` property to `amountAxis`.

Your code should appear as follows:

```
<mx:verticalAxis>
    <mx:LinearAxis id="amountAxis" title="Amount"
        minimum="0" maximum="500000"/>
</mx:verticalAxis>
<mx:verticalAxisRenderers>
    <mx:AxisRenderer verticalAxisTitleAlignment="vertical"
        axis="{amountAxis}"/>
</mx:verticalAxisRenderers>
```

Run the application. The vertical axis title is now rotated, as shown in Figure 6-12.

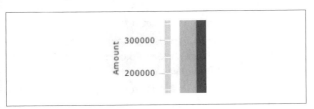

Figure 6-12. Rotate the vertical axis title

Step 4: Make the Axis Titles Bold

In *TestDrive.css*, create a ColumnChart type selector and set `axis-title-style-name` to a class selector called `brownTitles`. Create the class selector called `brownTitles` and set its `font-weight` to bold and its `color` to dark brown (#403029).

The selectors should appear as follows:

```
mx|ColumnChart
{
    axis-title-style-name:brownTitles;
}
.brownTitles
{
    font-weight:bold;
    color:#403029;
}
```

Run the application. The axis titles are now bold and brown.

Step 5: Set Axis and Tick Colors

Use the following steps to set the axis and tick colors to brown:

1. In the Declarations block, create a SolidColorStroke object called brownStrokeThick and set its color (#7F7364) and its weight (5).

2. Create a second SolidColorStroke object called brown StrokeThin and set its color (#7F7364) and its weight (1).

3. In the ColumnChart verticalAxisRenderers, set axis Stroke and tickStroke to the brownStrokeThick and brownStrokeThin objects.

4. Set the horizontalAxisRenderers property to an instance of the AxisRenderer class and set its axis to expen seAxis and its stroke styles the same as the other renderer.

The declarations should appear as follows:

```
<s:SolidColorStroke id="brownStrokeThick" color="#7F7364"
    weight="5"/>
<s:SolidColorStroke id="brownStrokeThin" color="#7F7364"
    weight="1"/>
```

The axis renderers should appear as follows:

```
<mx:verticalAxisRenderers>
    <mx:AxisRenderer verticalAxisTitleAlignment="vertical"
        axis="{amountAxis}" axisStroke="{brownStrokeThick}"
        tickStroke="{brownStrokeThin}"/>
```

```
    </mx:verticalAxisRenderers>
    <mx:horizontalAxisRenderers>
        <mx:AxisRenderer axis="{expenseAxis}"
            axisStroke="{brownStrokeThick}"
            tickStroke="{brownStrokeThin}"/>
    </mx:horizontalAxisRenderers>
```

Run the application. The axes and ticks are now brown, as
shown in Figure 6-13.

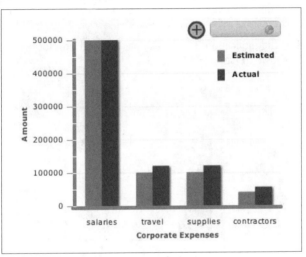

Figure 6-13. Change the axis and tick colors

Step 6: Format Axis Labels as Currencies

In the Declarations block, create a CurrencyFormatter called
moneyFormatter and set its properties to format in your currency. In the LinearAxis tag, set its labelFunction to
axisMoneyFormatter. In the Script block, include the following
formatter function:

```
    import mx.charts.chartClasses.IAxis;
    protected function axisMoneyFormatter(labelValue:Object,
        previousValue:Object, axis:IAxis):String{
```

```
        return moneyFormatter.format(labelValue);
}
```

The LinearAxis code should appear as follows:

```
<mx:LinearAxis id="amountAxis" title="Amount" minimum="0"
    maximum="500000" labelFunction="axisMoneyFormatter"/>
```

The chart component calls the formatter function for every label on the vertical axis. Its method signature (its arguments and return type) are defined by the component using it. You can look up the method's required signature in the API for the LinearAxis class.

Run the application. The vertical axis labels are now formatted, as shown in Figure 6-14.

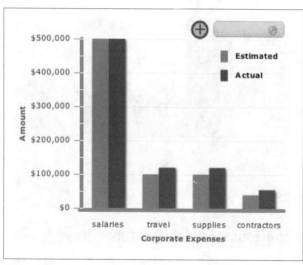

Figure 6-14. Format the vertical axis labels as currencies

Step 7: Format Data Tips

Set the PieChart `dataTipFunction` to `formatDeptPieTips`. In the `Script` block, include the following formatter function:

```
import mx.charts.HitData;
protected function
  formatDeptPieTips(hitData:HitData):String{
  return ""+hitData.item.name+""+"Budget: "
  +moneyFormatter.format(hitData.item.budget);
}
```

The `PieChart` opening tag should appear as follows:

```
<mx:PieChart includeIn="DepartmentChart,DepartmentDetails"
  x="35" y="308" id="deptPieCht" width="282" height="282"
  dataProvider="{deptDg.dataProvider}" showDataTips="true"
  itemClick="deptPieCht_itemClickHandler(event)"
  dataTipFunction="formatDeptPieTips">
```

The chart component calls the formatter function before displaying every data tip. Just as for the `labelFunction` in the last step, its method signature is defined by the component using it, the PieChart, and you can look it up in the API for that class.

NOTE

You can use only basic HTML formatting in this formatter function.

Run the application. The pie chart data tips are now formatted to display currency amounts, as shown in Figure 6-15.

Congratulations! In this module you've learned to add charts to your Flex application. You used a pie chart and a column chart and accomplished all the common customization tasks, including drilling down into data; animating data changes; and formatting fills, axes, titles, labels, and data tips.

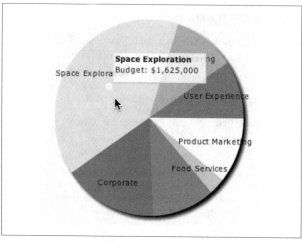

Figure 6-15. Format data tips

The completed code should look like the following (you can download the sample application at *www.adobe.com/devnet/flex/testdrive/assets/testdrive_add_charts.zip*):

TestDrive.mxml

```
<?xml version="1.0" encoding="utf-8"?>
<s:Application ...>
  <fx:Style source="TestDrive.css"/>
  <fx:Script>
    <![CDATA[
      (...)
      import mx.charts.HitData;
      import mx.charts.chartClasses.IAxis;
      import mx.charts.events.ChartItemEvent;
      import mx.charts.series.items.PieSeriesItem;

    protected function
      deptPieCht_itemClickHandler(
        event:ChartItemEvent):void
    {
      currentState="DepartmentDetails";
      deptColCht.dataProvider=
        createDataProvider(event.hitData.item);
```

```
      expenseAxis.title=
        event.hitData.item.name+" Expenses";
      estSeries.setStyle("fill",(event.hitData.chartItem
        as PieSeriesItem).fill);
    }
    protected function
      axisMoneyFormatter(labelValue:Object,
        previousValue:Object, axis:IAxis):String{
        return moneyFormatter.format(labelValue);
        }

      protected function
        formatDeptPieTips(hitData:HitData):String{
          return"<b>"+hitData.item.name+"</b><br/>"+
          "Budget: "+moneyFormatter.format(
          hitData.item.budget);
      }
    ]]>
</fx:Script>
<fx:Declarations>
   (...)
   <mx:SeriesInterpolate id="interpolate"
     duration="1000"/>
   <s:SolidColorStroke id="brownStrokeThick"
     color="#7F7364" weight="5"/>
   <s:SolidColorStroke id="brownStrokeThin"
     color="#7F7364" weight="1"/>
   <mx:CurrencyFormatter id="moneyFormatter"
     currencySymbol="$" precision="0"/>
</fx:Declarations>
(...)
<mx:PieChart
  includeIn="DepartmentChart,DepartmentDetails" x="35"
  y="308" id="deptPieCht" width="282" height="282"
  dataProvider="{deptDg.dataProvider}"
  itemClick="deptPieCht_itemClickHandler(event)"
  showDataTips="true"
  dataTipFunction="formatDeptPieTips">
  <mx:series>
     <mx:PieSeries field="budget" nameField="name"
       labelField="name" labelPosition="inside" />
  </mx:series>
</mx:PieChart>
<mx:ColumnChart includeIn="DepartmentDetails" x="325"
  y="308" id="deptColCht" height="278" width="363"
  showDataTips="true">
  <mx:horizontalAxis>
```

```
            <mx:CategoryAxis id="expenseAxis" title="Expenses"
              categoryField="field"/>
         </mx:horizontalAxis>
         <mx:verticalAxis>
            <mx:LinearAxis id="amountAxis" title="Amount"
              minimum="0" maximum="500000"
              labelFunction="axisMoneyFormatter"/>
         </mx:verticalAxis>
         <mx:verticalAxisRenderers>
            <mx:AxisRenderer
              verticalAxisTitleAlignment="vertical"
              axis="{amountAxis}"
              axisStroke="{brownStrokeThick}"
              tickStroke="{brownStrokeThin}"/>
         </mx:verticalAxisRenderers>
         <mx:horizontalAxisRenderers>
            <mx:AxisRenderer axis="{expenseAxis}"
              axisStroke="{brownStrokeThick}"
              tickStroke="{brownStrokeThin}"/>
         </mx:horizontalAxisRenderers>
         <mx:series>
            <mx:ColumnSeries  id="estSeries"
              displayName="Estimated" yField="est"
              showDataEffect="{interpolate}"/>
            <mx:ColumnSeries  displayName="Actual"
              yField="actual" showDataEffect="{interpolate}"
              styleName="brownFill"/>
         </mx:series>
      </mx:ColumnChart>
      <mx:Legend includeIn="DepartmentDetails"
        dataProvider="{deptColCht}" x="596" y="325"/>
      <!--<mx:Legend includeIn="DepartmentChart"
        dataProvider="{deptPieCht}" x="323" y="308"/>-->
   </s:Application>
```

TestDrive.css

```
   mx|PieSeries
   {
     fills:#7F7364,#BFB59F,#E5DFC3,#586F99,#6782B2,#ADCAFF,
     #F8F8F4;
   }
   .brownFill
   {
     fill:#403029;
   }
   mx|ColumnChart
```

```
{
  axis-title-style-name:brownTitles;
}
.brownTitles
{
  font-weight:bold;
  color:#403029;
}
```

This concludes your test drive of Flash Builder 4. In less than a day, you've learned to build a Flex application that retrieves, displays, updates, adds, and deletes data in a database, and you learned to debug, deploy, customize, and add charts to this application. The finished application is shown in Figure 6-16.

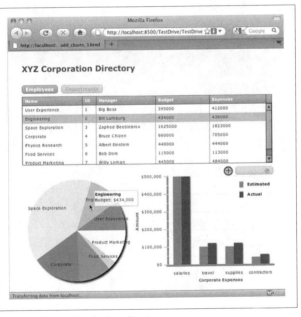

Figure 6-16. The finished application

CHAPTER 7

Resources for Flex Developers

There are many ways you can learn about Flex. This chapter highlights a few select resources. As you explore these resources, you will surely discover even more sources of information.

The Adobe Flex Developer Center (*www.adobe.com/devnet/flex/*) is the official Adobe Flex community center and has articles and great information for Flex developers.

Online Resources for Getting Started

There are many ways to get started with Flex:

Flex Test Drive (www.adobe.com/devnet/flex/testdrive/)
Quickly build an application with Flex.

Flex in a Week (www.adobe.com/devnet/flex/videotraining/)
A free one-week video training course in Flex.

Flex QuickStarts (www.adobe.com/devnet/flex/quickstarts/)
Dozens of examples with code explaining a broad range of topics, including application basics, handling data, and building advanced user interfaces.

Tour de Flex (www.adobe.com/devnet/flex/tourdeflex/)
A desktop application with over 200 running samples with source code. Tour de Flex showcases Flex capabilities and resources.

*Flex documentation (www.adobe.com/devnet/flex/?view=docu
mentation)*
>   Provides access to all Flex and Flex-related documenta-
>   tion from Adobe.

Adobe TV (http://tv.adobe.com/product/flex/)
>   A collection of video learning resources from Adobe.

The Flex Cookbook

The Adobe Flex Cookbook is an invaluable resource for both
Flex beginners and experienced Flex coders. It's a community-
driven repository of code fragments for Flex that solves lots of
common coding problems. If you are stumped about how to
do something, the first place to visit is the Flex Cookbook
(*www.adobe.com/go/flex_cookbook*).

When you have something to contribute, you can add recipes
to the Cookbook and reap the benefits of participating in a very
active Flex community.

The Flex Cookbook home page even offers an Eclipse plug-in
that shows you the most recent Cookbook entries in Flex
Builder.

Community Links and Resources

Flex blogs are a primary source of information about Flex.
Often, blog entries include code recipes that are too small to
warrant coverage in an article but are nonetheless helpful and
can save you the time and effort of researching and imple-
menting Flex solutions yourself.

Here's a list of some of the best Flex blogs and community
websites:

Flex Team Blog (http://blogs.adobe.com/flex/)
>   This is the official blog from the Flex team at Adobe.

Peter deHaan (http://blog.flexexamples.com/)

Peter deHaan is a member of the Flex SDK team. His blog provides examples on using and customizing Flex components.

Mike Morearty (www.morearty.com/blog/)

Mike Morearty is the brains behind the debugging portion of Flex Builder. His blog keeps you up-to-date on what's happening in the world of Flex.

Chet Haase (http://graphics-geek.blogspot.com/)

Chet Haase's blog specializes in Flex/Flash graphics techniques.

Alex Harui (http://blogs.adobe.com/aharui/)

Alex Harui's Flex Closet is a collection of Flex-related things. The blog contains numerous demos and down-loadable source files.

Sujit Reddy G (http://sujitreddyg.wordpress.com/)

Sujit Reddy is a technical evangelist for Flash Platform technologies at Adobe. His blog contains examples and tutorials on accessing data with Flex and Flash Builder.

Adobe Feeds (http://feeds.adobe.com/)

Adobe Feeds is a blog aggregator that you can use to search for articles on Flex and Flash Builder. As a starting point, under Smart Categories choose Flex.

RIAForge (http://www.riaforge.org/)

This site hosts several open source development projects for Flex.

Flex.org (http://flex.org)

This is the Flex community website.

InsideRIA (http://www.insideria.com/)

This is O'Reilly's RIA website.

Flex Support Forums

A great community resource is the Flex Support Forums (*http://forums.adobe.com/community/flex*), where you can find user-to-user discussions regarding Flex. What's more, the Flex team monitors the forums to help you out when you get into a jam.

Adobe Community Help Client (CHC)

The CHC, which is installed with Flash Builder, provides a portal to Adobe Flex documentation and a variety of Adobe and nonAdobe learning content. The CHC provides search options that include both Adobe and community resources, plus user feedback. The CHC can filter searches for resources containing code samples. If you don't have Flash Builder installed yet or you want to check out the next-generation help experience from Adobe for Flash Builder or any other product, visit *www.adobe.com/support/chc/*.

FlexCoders

The FlexCoders Yahoo! group (*http://tech.groups.yahoo .com/group/flexcoders/*) is an active forum where experienced Flex developers ask questions and exchange ideas.

Social networking

Follow Flex on Facebook and Twitter to access the latest examples, videos, and news. Access Flex on Facebook at *www.facebook.com/adobeflex*. On Twitter, search for *#flex* and *#flashbuilder*.

Flex user groups

It's a good idea to join a local Flex user group. Flex user groups are located all over the world and are cataloged at *http://groups.adobe.com/*. Meanwhile, a Flex or Flash "Camp" (an informal gathering of Flex enthusiasts and Adobe folks who get together to try to build real Flex applications) should be high on your list of things to attend. Upcoming Flash Camp events are displayed prominently in the sidebar of the Adobe Groups page.

Newsletters

You should consider subscribing to *The Edge* (*http://www .adobe.com/newsletters/edge/*), Adobe's newsletter for designers and developers.

The *News Flash* newsletter (*http://www.adobe.com/devnet/ria/newsletter/index.html*) is a free publication to help developers to stay current with the latest news about the Adobe Flash Platform.

Books

Besides this book, there are many books on Flex 4 and ActionScript 3 currently available. Check out the *Flex 4 Cookbook* by Joshua Noble et al. (O'Reilly, *http://oreilly.com/catalog/9780596805623*). Its sister publication, *ActionScript 3.0 Cookbook*, by Joey Lott et al. (O'Reilly, *http://oreilly.com/catalog/9780596526955/*) is also an excellent resource. Colin Moock's *Essential ActionScript 3.0* (O'Reilly, *http://oreilly.com/catalog/9780596526948/*), demonstrates use of ActionScript that will blow your mind.

You can also check *http://oreilly.com/flex/index.html* and *http://flex.org* for lists of books and other resources for Flex developers.

Index

We'd like to hear your suggestions for improving our indexes. Send email to
index@oreilly.com.

Colophon

The animal on the cover of *Getting Started with Flex*™ *4* is a sea urchin. The name is generic—"urcheon" is Middle English for "hedgehog"—and covers members of the taxonomic class *Echinoidea*. Sea urchins can be found in every ocean and in a wide range of colors, including black, green, brown, purple, and red. Specimens are typically small, only growing to 1–4 inches across, though some extraordinary urchins have been found measuring 14 inches across.

Sea urchins possess fivefold symmetry, similar to sand dollars and sea stars, though it is often not immediately apparent in living individuals. Their shells, called tests, are round and spiny, and their small tube feet allow them to move slowly along surfaces, gathering food into their downward-facing mouths. Sea urchins eat mostly algae, but will sometimes also eat various invertebrates such as mussels and sponges. Reproduction occurs externally; both sperm and eggs are released into the sea water, where fertilization occurs. A fertilized sea urchin egg can develop into a free-swimming embryo in as little as 12 hours, though it may take several months for the individual to develop from that stage to its adult form.

The ovaries of a sea urchin, called corals or roe, are considered a delicacy in many parts of the world. Though prepared differently and from different species, sea urchin are eaten in the Mediterranean, Chile, the West Indies, New Zealand, the Pacific coast of North America, and Japan, for example. The demand for sea urchin is particularly high in Japan, where high-quality *uni*, as it is called, can sell for as much as $450/kg.

The cover image is from *Johnson's Natural History*. The cover font is Adobe ITC Garamond. The text font is Linotype Birka; the heading font is Adobe Myriad Condensed; and the code font is LucasFont's TheSansMonoCondensed.

Buy this book and get access to the online edition for 45 days—for free!

Getting Started with Flex 4
By Jeanette Stallons, Andrew Shorten & Vince Genovese
September 2010, $14.99
ISBN 9780596804114

To try out Safari and the online edition of this book FREE for 45 days, go to **oreilly.com/go/safarienabled** and enter the coupon code FOHJZAA. To see the complete Safari Library, visit safari.oreilly.com.

With Safari Books Online, you can:

Access the contents of thousands of technology and business books

- Quickly search over 7000 books and certification guides
- Download whole books or chapters in PDF format, at no extra cost, to print or read on the go
- Copy and paste code
- Save up to 35% on O'Reilly print books
- **New!** Access mobile-friendly books directly from cell phones and mobile devices

Stay up-to-date on emerging topics before the books are published

- Get on-demand access to evolving manuscripts.
- Interact directly with authors of upcoming books

Explore thousands of hours of video on technology and design topics

- Learn from expert video tutorials
- Watch and replay recorded conference sessions

O'REILLY®

Spreading the knowledge of innovators   oreilly.com